CALLED TO SERVE
LIFE AS A FIREFIGHTER-DEACON

DEACON ANTHONY R. SUROZENSKI

BARNABAS BOOKS

Called to Serve: Life as a Firefighter-Deacon
Copyright © 2011 Anthony R. Surozenski

Published by Barnabas Books
An imprint of Winged Lion Press
Hamden, CT

Winged Lion Press titles may be purchased for business or promotional use or special sales.

10-9-8-7-6-5-4-3-2-1

ISBN-13 978-1-936294-07-7

"This book provides a rare glimpse into the life of a fire chaplain. However, Tony shows us something more – the heart, mind and soul of his personal life."
Sandy Scerra
Massachusetts Peer Support Network, Coordinator
International Critical Incident Stress Foundation, Faculty

"As a former chief and firefighter, the stories brought back memories of how things were done in the "good old days" when air packs were a luxury. They also reveal struggles that we all had from time to time with facing the reality of tragic moments and how we handled them. It certainly is an interesting read. A firefighter/chaplain is a blessing to the fire service. He has been there and knows where the firefighters are coming from."
Former Chief Gordon D. Wentworth
Webster Fire

"Deacon Tony Surozenski looks at the fire service from a number of angles, each one offering useful and important lessons. He began as a firefighter, rising to the rank of Captain. When he was ordained as a Roman Catholic deacon, Tony became a fire chaplain, noting how his role evolved over time. As a member of the Massachusetts Corps of Fire Chaplains he has responded to some of the largest incidents in our recent history. His experience and storytelling expertise make this one book you must read!"
Rev. James A. Tilbe
Chief Chaplain, Massachusetts Corps of Fire Chaplains

"Chaplain Tony's account of his experience at the 9/11 site brought out the pain and grief that all firefighters felt after the attack. He also shows us through his own personal experience that we all have our own demons to bear."
Chief Gordon Forrester
Webster Fire

ACKNOWLEDGEMENTS

Without a loving family it would have been difficult to go through forty years of combined service as a teacher, firefighter, deacon, and chaplain. I thank God for a loving wife, Alice, who stuck by me through many difficult times. I am also thankful for Chuck, Jeff, and Jenn who have come to realize that it was just as difficult for their dad to leave in the middle of special events as it was for them to see him run off when he was called into service.

This book would not have been published if it were not for the encouragement of former Chief Chaplain and currently bishop of the Episcopal Diocese of Long Island New York, Larry Provenzano and the support of the members of the Massachusetts Corps of Fire Chaplains. He was also instrumental in contacting Karen McCarthy who did the proof reading and editing. She was a great help in making things flow more smoothly and an easier read. I am very grateful for all of their help and support.

I also thank my darling daughter Jennifer for taking the time to make the corrections that were noted by Karen and for re-typing the final document.

I would be remiss if I did not note how grateful I am for having parents who raised me to become a person of service to family, church, and community.

Gratitude goes out to my brother Richard, who was always there for my parents in time of need. The lack of worry about my parents allowed the freedom to become the deacon-chaplain of service.

A special thanks to a high school friend, David Rybacki, who launched my carrier in the fire services. And, a thank you to the first firefighter and his wife, who befriended us from the very beginning and are still friends to this day, Peter and Shirley LaCerte.

Credit goes to Alan Bracket of "First Due Images" for the cover photographs and several interior photographs.

Credit is also given to The Worcester Telegram & Gazette, the Catholic Free Press, and the MCFC, Stonebridge Press & Webster Times for the photographs as noted within. And thanks to Carla Manzi of the web site Olde Webster and to Former Chief Gordon D. Wentworth and his son, Lt. Gordon Wentworth for their assistance with gathering the prints.

And finally, a heartfelt thanks for the kind words of those who endorsed the project and to all who contributed to my training as a teacher, firefighter, deacon, chaplain, and CISM instructor.

May God's blessings rest upon all.

DEDICATION

This compilation of stories is dedicated both to those men and women of the fire services who risk their lives daily for the protection of life and property, and is also in a special way, dedicated to those who offer their prayers and presence to all who are in need of a healthy body, mind, and spirit, the Fire Chaplains.

May the God of their faith guide and protect them all as they perform their service of love.

FROM GROUND LADDERS TO TOWERS – ALL IN A DAY'S WORK

East Main and Wakefield - Webster, Massachusettes

Called to Serve

INTRODUCTION

The following pages are filled with stories about a person, who, from a very early age, fell in love with fire trucks and with those people who were called firefighters. He always dreamed of becoming one and eventually did. He actually became a call firefighter and, later on in his career, was appointed as the department Fire Chaplain. It was a strange twist of fate that led him from being a college student who worked in a mill to help pay for his education, to being a teacher/firefighter, then a masonry laborer to help make extra money for the family, then a teacher/firefighter/deacon, then a teacher/deacon/fire chaplain, then a retired teacher, and then a deacon/fire chaplain.

His love for the fire services helped him to become a better person. It helped to prepare him for a life of service in the Catholic Church as a deacon and at the same time to remain in the service of those whom he admired and grew to love. They were and are the men and women of the fire service.

No names are mentioned in the stories. It is the author's wish to have the readers place themselves in the position of those involved so as to get a feel for the experience at the time (1960-2007). The author hopes that all will enjoy the stories. May the reader grow to love all who are in the fire service. And, may the God of your faith bless you as you read.

Tony

Fire Chaplain/Deacon

WATCH OUT UNDERFOOT!!!

HIGH STREET GARAGE FIRE - WEBSTER, MASSACHUSETTES

CALLED TO SERVE

IT'S ONLY A GARAGE FIRE

It was evening and all call firefighters who had any training sessions had gone home. The temperature was hovering around zero degrees Celsius and the rain began to fall, causing the ground and roadways to be covered with a thin coating of ice. It was a crystal wonderland to some but not for those in the emergency services. The local highway department had just started to send out the sanders when the phone call came in to police dispatch that there was a garage on fire with a vehicle in the garage. Box 442 was struck as the tones went off for all fire personnel to report to the station.

A police cruiser was dispatched to the location but was delayed because it slid down the icy road several hundred feet and ended up near a set of railroad tracks at the bottom of the hill. It passed the intersection where the road to the fire scene crossed. Due to the expert driving skill of the officer behind the wheel, he was not injured nor was there any damage to his cruiser. Immediately, the police officer notified all who were en route of the icy conditions.

About the same time the deputy chief signed on and gave the order to proceed with caution at a reduced rate of speed. Within a short time thereafter the first engine company began its trek over the treacherous roads. A second engine responded along with Ladder Two and Rescue.

The local fire chaplain was monitoring the call and said a quick prayer for all who were traveling to the station and scene to be safe. Usually he would respond on second alarm assignments but, of course, this was only a garage fire and these are not usually too eventful.

DEACON TONY SUROZENSKI

He would like to think that his prayers would be answered, and according to the chatter over the radio it didn't appear as though the situation was getting out of hand, nor that the adjacent structure was in danger of catching on fire. It wasn't until several days later that the chaplain found out just how his prayers were answered.

According to the fire report, a wood-burning stove was over-stoked causing heat to reach to a dangerous level, and it transferred to the adjacent walls which reached their kindling temperature, causing the wooden walls to burst into flames. However, this was not the main problem. Believe it or not, an old-style fire extinguisher that was standing a few feet away from the stove began to heat up. The relief valve didn't activate which led to a "BLEVE." (Boiling Liquid Expanding Vapor Explosion) The result sent the extinguisher bouncing all over the garage.

At one point it was driven under the vehicle that was parked in the garage and the sharp jagged metal tore a hole in the gasoline tank which caused yet another explosion. To add insult to injury, the oxyacetylene tank's valves released, sending their gases into the mix. This happened within minutes as several firefighters were about to advance the hose line into the side entrance of the garage.

If it were not for the icy road conditions which slowed the entire operation down, at least five men would have been inside the structure when all hell broke loose. "It's only a garage fire" could have led to a bagpipe procession and several funerals. Were the chaplain's prayers answered? Let the reader decide.

CRYSTAL BALL OR COINCIDENCE?

Many interesting things happen to all in the fire service whether they are volunteer, paid-call, or regular municipal fire departments. Here's one that is a bit eerie.

One evening, while on break from his usual work in a woolen mill, one of the firefighters was amused by one of the ladies and her little toy game. It was nothing more than a small cardboard square with a "yes" at the top and bottom and a "no" to the left and right edges of the square. With this came a glass "crystal" ball that was attached to a fairly thick string.

According to the lady, if you held the string in your finger tips and rested your elbow outside the square while adjusting the glass ball slightly above the square and keeping it in the center, you could ask questions and the ball would swing around. If it swung from top to bottom, that would mean "yes" to your answer, and if it went from side to side, that meant "no." If it went in a circular motion, that would mean "maybe."

Everyone around her seemed to have fun with the game. They would ask questions about being married and if they were going to have any more kids or not. Laughter surrounded the area. Well, when it came to the firefighter's turn, he asked a very direct question. "Is there going to be a fire tonight?" The pendulum-type thread and ball moved from top to bottom indicating "yes."

The next question was, "Will I be going to the fire?" The pendulum swung to the top and then to the bottom and the fire alarm could be heard bellowing out its usual air horn sound. The faces of all who witnessed the situation widened in amazement as the firefighter rushed off to his vehicle to get to the fire.

It turned out to be a two-story structure fire with flames rising up from one side and moving up to the second floor and roof. At that time, the firefighters kept their "rubber goods," protective turn out gear, tied onto the apparatus. Wouldn't you know, the firefighter's gear was on a truck that hadn't responded. Have no fear, work clothes are old and if destroyed, it shouldn't be a big problem. Helmet? Not necessary if you are climbing up a ladder. You only need one on the inside to protect your head from falling ceiling plaster. Air pack? Those are the new things that only sissies use. Real firefighters eat smoke and cough a little. Besides, after all the coughing and spitting, you just sit on the back of a rig, light up a cigarette, relax and maybe cough a little from the cigarette. No biggie. Oh, the good old days with no plastics or serious toxic fumes. All that burned was just wood, paper, cloth, and maybe some leather.

Fortunately, it was a quick knock-down and all over within an hour or so. Back to work for the firefighter where anxious ears awaited the news of all that happened. The boss was the first to greet the firefighter and called him into his office where he listened with the awe of a young boy who wanted to be a fireman.

The plant owners never fired a fireman even though they missed an hour or so of work now and then. It was an unwritten law of all who owned businesses where firefighters were employed to allow the firemen to leave work and get to the fire. In some workplaces, this could be a real problem if several of the workers were firefighters. Once in a while there would be complaints, but in general, all were let loose to put the "wet stuff on the red stuff." Who knew? Maybe one day it could have been the owner's home and he or she certainly would be thankful for following that unwritten rule.

(NOTE TO THE READER: THE AUTHOR DOES NOT ENDORSE ANY SUCH GAMES BECAUSE THEY CAN INVOKE OCCULT SPIRITS. OFTEN TIMES, A GAME THAT SEEMS TO BE HARMLESS CAN BECOME DANGEROUS TO ONE'S SOUL. THIS WAS A ONETIME EVENT IN HIS LIFE AND HIS SENSE WAS TO NEVER ENGAGE IN THIS TYPE OF PLAY EVER AGAIN. FOR THOSE INTERESTED IN FINDING OUT MORE ABOUT GAMES AND THE OCCULT, THE INTERNET HAS SEVERAL GOOD SITES TO EXPLORE.)

TAKING ADVANTAGE OF A GOOD THING

Once in a while there is someone in the fire service who pushes the limit and gets into a little trouble. Case in point. One late spring afternoon a box alarm came in to the local firehouse for a structure fire. The caller said that they could see smoke coming out of a building that housed apartments on the upper level and a bar and restaurant on the lower level, with storage in the basement. "No flames showing" was heard over the fire radios.

The first alarm assignment quickly turned into a second alarm simply to get the manpower and apparatus on the scene. A ladder was set up to get ready to vent the roof, hydrants were tapped, and crews were inside the building trying to locate the source of the smoke. A light white haze filled the inside stairwells.

Firefighters felt the walls with bare hands to feel any heat coming from within (no "thermal imaging" devices back then). Some could hear crackling in the walls and it seemed to be moving quickly from one floor to the next. An Assistant Chief came in with handkerchief bunched up next to his face. This was his filtration system, a substitute for the new air packs. Of course, several of the old timers had their handkerchiefs out, too.

The Assistant Chief quickly sensed that something was just not right, ordered the men out of the building, ran outside, and looked up at the eaves only to find the dreaded signs of smoke being sucked back into the building. He gave the word to sound the alarm and every truck on the scene blasted air horns and let their sirens wail. The ladder men abandoned their efforts to vent the roof and headed back down the 75-foot ladder. At the same time, the last two men were just about to exit the building when the back draft took effect and blew the two right out the doorway and into the wall of the adjacent structure. Helmets and rubber goods came in handy that day. Looking back, the two men said that it was somewhat comical because their feet were moving in a running motion but they were several inches above the ground and still moving forward. The brick wall stopped them from going any further. It couldn't have been too bad because they caught each other and stopped themselves from falling over. They chuckled a bit and couldn't believe what they had just experienced. Later on, they realized how bad it could have been.

The fire quickly spread throughout the structure but was eventually extinguished due to a combination of interior and exterior attacks. Now came the good part. The reason? If you were able to be on standby duty, you could get paid extra and have a pretty relaxing evening. Once in a while a hot spot would flare up but a little dowse from an inch-and-a-half line did the trick. Walking through the building could, at times, be adventurous and quite interesting especially when it came to a restaurant, a bar, with food and liquor. Hmmm.

That evening, one of the firefighters got the bright idea of investigating the freezer section to see if anything could be salvaged. No fruitful situation there. Interesting, though, that the backs of lobsters were red and the middle and bottoms were green. A little foam would make for an interesting Newburg sauce. No food salvage, though; it was too dangerous when one thought of all the bacteria and chemical infusions that could be floating around the scene. However, sealed bottles looked pretty good. A couple of men reasoned that the bottles would be brought to the local dump and be destroyed. What a waste (no pun intended). And, they also remembered that the owner said that they could take whatever was salvageable, for themselves. So they began to place bottles of various types of liquor in their boots and rubber goods and carried them off to the waiting compartments of a big red truck.

A few weeks later, a great company party was had by all; that is, all who were on the Hose Company that was on standby night duty throughout that eventful night.

Walking through the building to make sure there are no smoldering hot spots can be tedious at best, and then the morning cleanup with the rolling of hoses, breaking open the couplings, and stacking the fifty-foot lengths of two-and-a-half and inch-and-a-half hoses really tires one out. How does a person go to work that day and do an effective job without the needed sleep of the previous night? As they say, "It ain't easy." But there are those who do it time and time again in the fire service.

However, once in a while, you may get a firefighter who is able to take time off as a sick day. Now, that was an idea that one of the paid call firefighters had, who happened to be a school teacher. He got the bright idea of being able to get paid for the extra duty, call in sick, and get paid for being able to sleep throughout part of the next day.

It did work, but not exactly the way he thought it would. While he was teaching a science class the following day, he received an unexpected visit from the Superintendent of Schools. This man pulled no punches and was very direct. He simply asked. "Do you want to be an 'Fn' firefighter or a school teacher? Tell me right now." Of course the teacher knew that his full-time job paid the bills, so he said that he wanted to be a school teacher, even though, deep down in his heart, his real love was for the fire service.

After the teacher's response, the Superintendent then said "Good choice. You do a good job here. Don't pull that shit again. Now get back in there and teach those kids some science." After giving it some thought, the teacher/firefighter began to say bravely in his mind " 'F' you pal, but if it was your house or business, I'll bet you would think differently about it." Fortunately for him, he kept his thoughts to himself. As a result, the teacher/firefighter was able to do both jobs for many more years and worked his way to becoming Captain of Ladder One and even more.

DEACON TONY SUROZENSKI

13

As fire broke through twin spires of Sts. Constantine and Helen Greek Orthodox Church, Firefighters used the aerial ladder truck to pour water into the burning edifice.

FIRE SHOWS NO MERCY

COURTESY WEBSTER TIMES

HOLY SMOKE

Ask any firefighter and they will tell you that one of the most difficult fires to bring under control is a fire that has had a good start in an old church. Balloon framing and the natural chimney effect of the steeples are a tremendous help in getting the fire to climb and spread throughout the church quickly. Lightning does a fine job of striking steeples, following electrical wires, and igniting whatever is in its path. This is just the thing that happened one warm afternoon.

A local Orthodox Church caught fire following a thunderstorm. Before anyone realized what had happened, smoke began to billow out through the roof and steeples. Even though the firehouse was located just down the street and the response time was reasonably quick, due to the fact that many firemen lived within a few minutes' drive from the station, the church was too far gone to be saved.

It wasn't quite a 'surround and drown' type of situation, but it was pretty close. Several engine companies came up the narrow roadway from different directions, tapping into different hydrants. One came to the scene before the hydrant and the Officer called for a "full reverse." In those days they didn't have ready lines, Mattydales, pre-connected hoses to an engine's pump, and the like, so the firefighters who rode the step would jump off, disconnect the coupling from the gates that were attached to the hoses that would normally be wrapped around the hydrant and eventually connected, change them to double male connections, attach the nozzles, pull out the estimated lengths of hose needed to work the fire, and then call for the truck to roll.

When the truck got to the hydrant, double female connections were attached to the hoses. Then the hoses were attached to the gates, and finally, the gates with the hoses attached were connected to the hydrants. The usual ten to fifteen turns of the hydrant wrench in a clockwise direction brought water gushing through the hydrant and up to the gates. When the call for water was given, the gates were open and the water moved through the flat, hoses filling them with a crackling/popping type noise and moving them from side to side as the water moved toward the nozzles.

There was not much by way of radio communications back then. Loud voices screaming orders could be heard everywhere. Specific commands were a must. "Water on line one from Engine One... Water from Hose Two...Attach the Deck Gun...Get that Ladder Pipe ready...Vent the roof." These and similar orders were yelled out by men on the line, drivers, and officers, depending upon who was where and what was needed at the time.

At this church fire, lines were taken around the back and sides. A water curtain was set up to protect an adjacent home. At one point an interior attack was made from the front and a line was advanced up a stairwell to the choir loft. Eventually the interior attack was stopped due to the danger involved. A ladder pipe was attached to the seventy-five foot ladder of Ladder One. The ladder was raised over the now-collapsed steeple and roof, and water was poured into the building.

The firefighter at the pipe controlled the up and down motion of the pipe with the handle that was attached to it. He also was able to attach a rope and tie it off at the upper rungs when he needed to do so. Fortunately there was radio communication between the pipe man and the ladder man at the operations console. The Pipe man could signal down to have the ladder moved from left to right or elevated or lowered as he saw fit.

In this case, as in so many others, an overnight watch was called for. Often Auxiliary firefighters were offered an opportunity to serve. This was a good way to eventually become a "Regular." Friendships developed along with trust between the Auxiliaries and the Regulars. And, yes, there is always one in the crowd. An Auxiliary asked the driver in charge if this is what was meant by, you guessed it, "Holy Smoke?"

Fortunately for the congregation, some of the sacred icons and vessels were saved. A new church was eventually constructed at a different site.

DEACON TONY SUROZENSKI

CHIEFS, READY FOR ACTION?

27 MECHANIC STREET - WEBSTER, MASSACHUSETTES

CALLED TO SERVE

SHE AIN'T GONNA FIT THROUGH THAT WINDOW

It was around 10:00 A.M. one morning and a box alarm sounded, signifying a possible structure fire on North Main St. As it turned out, one of the firefighters lived nearby, donned his "Bunker Coat" and boots, saw the smoke through the trees that rose above the house across the street, and proceeded to run over to the fire.

A very full-bodied pregnant lady had her head and upper body extended out a second-story window of a fully- involved duplex and was yelling for help. Other children were inside. No trucks were on the scene as yet and the horns could still be heard bellowing their second round. A police officer pulled up with his cruiser and noticed the woman in the window. He immediately swung his vehicle over the sidewalk and positioned it directly below the window in the hope that the woman would be able to get onto it. He bravely jumped on top of the roof of his cruiser and tried to coax her out.

The problem was that she was just too big in the ninth month of her pregnancy. Fortunately, the main bulk of the fire was in the opposite apartment of the duplex. Her side of the building was mostly filled with smoke. However, the fire was slowly spreading to the stairwell of her side. She screamed that it was getting hotter and more smoke was pouring in under the doors.

Shortly after this, trucks began to arrive on the scene, and the firefighter who arrived first grabbed an extension ladder from the side of the engine and with the help of another firefighter was able to lean it into the building, just below the open window. The lady couldn't get out but was able to hand the children to the firefighter on the ladder.

DEACON TONY SUROZENSKI

19

Once they were down, he attempted to get her out but she was just too big. He then went inside and up the stairwell to see if he could help her get out that way. The firefighter noticed that the railing and stairwell were now involved and did not want to take the chance of getting her out that way.

He immediately went inside the upper apartment and tried to get her out that window but was unable to. The only thing left to do was to have the firefighter, who was then on the ladder, break the picture window which was adjacent to the smaller windows. This allowed the ladder to be moved and the lady was assisted down the ladder to safety.

By this time, the fire had been knocked down and under control. Interior attacks on both floors and sides were made. While the rescue attempt was being made on the right side of the duplex, another one was being made on the left side on the first floor level. A youngster was trapped inside and an all-out effort was being made to locate and save the child. Unfortunately, the child was not found; the rescue attempts failed. They began the search for the body. One of the firefighters noticed what looked like the leg of a doll underneath a piece of sheetrock that had been taken down in the overhaul/search operation. He just kicked it and thought nothing of it. Later on, he found out that it had been the child.

Even though the Chief and others told him that even if he had recognized that it was the child and he were to have started CPR, those extra five minutes would not have made any difference. However, it still bothered him and ate at his guts. In other words, it made him psychologically sick to his stomach.

It continued to bother him for many years, even though he thought he had suppressed it in his mind. Often, firefighters simply "suck up" what they experience and move on with their lives and chalk it up as part of the job. Sometimes things surface later in life, however. In the earlier years of firefighting there was no such thing as CISM, Critical Incident Stress Management. Or was there?

Maybe the bending of elbows and the lifting of mugs at the local bar along with talking about the events of the fire was a type of stress management; at least the talking part, anyway.

HOW CAN WE PREVENT THIS FROM HAPPENING AGAIN?

COURTESY-WORCESTER TELEGRAM & GAZETTE

SMOKE DETECTORS ARE A MUST IN EVERY HOME

DEACON TONY SUROZENSKI

NOT JUST YOUR USUAL NUISANCE CALL
– HAPPY NEW YEAR, FOLKS

Every city and town seems to have their share of daily, weekly, or monthly nuisance calls, the calls that over a period of time the firefighters simply shrug off as "Oh, here we go again. Somebody burnt the toast at the housing for the elderly project." These usually come in at certain times of the day corresponding to meal times: the burnt toast, eggs, hot dogs, hamburgers, or other foods that would trigger the smoke alarms at various complexes.

In some cases the nuisance calls come in regularly at industrial plants. At one particular industrial plant the box alarm would come in at a specific time and day, due to a drop in water pressure within the building which affected the sprinkler system. "Here we go again: box 9 at the freaking Industrial Complex," would be the usual comment. After a while, hardly anyone would show up at the station house to answer the call. Usually, the security people at the plant would phone in to dispatch that it was a false alarm.

The company would try all kinds of things to correct the situation but after a while the same old thing would happen and the box would sound out and the tape at the firehouse would show "four rounds of eight holes." Thirty-two blasts of the horn can be trying on anyone within earshot. Even the townspeople would know that it was a false alarm at the Industrial Complex.

But on January 1, 1969, in the early hours of the morning, box 8 came in and it was not a false alarm. It was not your usual fire, either. The sky was lit with an orange glow that could be seen for miles. Mutual aid was called from surrounding towns and from a radius of twenty miles.

One firefighter looked out his bedroom window and could see the orange glow. It looked as if it was just one street over instead of the mile up the road that it actually was. Due to the optical illusion, the firefighter ran up the road only to realize that he was about halfway there and no truck was on the scene yet. Shortly thereafter, the first truck arrived. The men tapped into a hydrant and the truck took off, dropping several hundred feet of two-and-a-half inch diameter line. Flames and smoke were billowing out the roof and windows with fire brands being pushed all over the place.

The sub-zero temperature did not help the situation any. Fingers were numb and the firefighters' faces were attacked by a biting wind. When Hose 2 arrived with its deck gun, it was immediately sent to the back of one of the buildings that was fully involved to set up using a pump house that was on site. Three two-and-a-half inch diameter lines fed the deck gun which was aimed at the southern exposure of the brick building.

The nozzle was alternated from the corner of the building on the south side to the corner of the southeast side. Then, at the point when the bricks turned from red, to pink, to white, and began to explode into a powder form, the deck gun nozzle was turned to the alleyway permanently, to set the stream as a water curtain to protect the adjacent building on the southeast side.

One minor problem occurred when the hose truck was set into place. Because the packing around the deck gun leaked, a fine spray went all over the cab and body of the truck. At one point it looked like a red igloo. It was all iced in and could not be moved without chopping a few inches of ice from around the vehicle. The driver was the one who ran up to the fire. He was commandeered by the Captain of the truck who drove it to the scene.

The Captain was instrumental in positioning the truck and its deck gun and went off to take care of other men who were attacking the fire from another position. Every so often the Captain would come by the truck to see if all was well with the driver. Once, he had to bang off all the ice around the door so that the driver could get out and stretch his legs.

DEACON TONY SUROZENSKI

23

The fire burned well into New Year's Day, and for several days thereafter. Hot spots were taken care of as soon as they were spotted. Fortunately no one was injured, but many people would be out of work for months to come.

Younger firefighters are told of the old box 8 fire to remind them that no matter how many times a nuisance call comes in at the same place, one day, it just might not be a false alarm. Hopefully, it would never come in at a housing for the elderly complex, a hospital, or a nursing home.

COURTESY OF THE WORCESTER TELEGRAM & GAZETTE

A VERY MEMORABLE NEW YEAR'S DAY FOR FIREFIGHTERS

COURTESY OF THE WORCESTER TELEGRAM & GAZETTE

DEACON TONY SUROZENSKI

25

CHISEL HIM OUT – HE NEEDS A BREAK

Courtesy of the Worcester Telegram & Gazette

OK 'DOC' SHE'S RIGHT OVER HERE

In the late sixties and early seventies, this small town had a privately owned ambulance service that was pretty much a "scoop and run" type of operation. The chief at the time operated a car dealership and garage service which just happened to be where the ambulance would run from. It was his ambulance service. It was also the time when first aid training was being increased: CPR, pressure bandages, slings, and traction were topics of conversation of many who were interested in Emergency Medical Services. EMT was coming into its own in nearby cities and towns. Some of the firefighters would carry a first aid kit in the trunk of their car, filled with a variety of different-sized bandages, some disinfectant, gauze pads of various sizes, ointments, slings and rolls of elastic bandage, tape, scissors, pins and the like. The containers for these kits ranged from the store-bought kind with a red cross on the outside, to small duffle bags, suitcases, and even empty ammunition boxes.

One particularly warm evening, one of the firefighters was coming home from a date and noticed a car off the road that was resting up against a tree. It obviously was an accident because he could see the skid marks on the roadway, the dirt torn up on the side of the road and the dent in the front of the car caused by the tree that must have mysteriously jumped out in front of it. The vehicle was leaning on an angle and resting part-way up an embankment. A little steam was emanating from under the hood and some fluids were on the ground. A slight smell of gasoline was detected but not enough to cause any anxiety. A cruiser had just arrived on the scene and the police officer was checking out the victim who was behind the wheel.

DEACON TONY SUROZENSKI

As the firefighter emerged from his vehicle with his first aid kit in hand, he began to run towards the accident scene and heard the police officer yell out, "Over here, doc. Quickly, over here." The first aid kit must have reminded the police officer of a doctor's bag. Well, the firefighter went about his business of checking out the victim and placing bandages where they were needed to stop the bleeding around the face and upper torso. A hip seemed to be out of place so when the ambulance did come, all were involved in doing their best to lay the person in so the hip would not be damaged any further. "Scoop and run" was the next order of business and off to the local hospital they went: ambulance driver, 'doc,' and patient. All went well in the emergency room, with compliments paid to 'doc' for a job well done. The police played taxi and gave the firefighter a ride back to his vehicle. It was all in a day's work for 'doc.'

SHORT-LIVED 'DOC'

Even after only a few years of ambulance runs and scenes that most folks couldn't talk about, some in the EMS business come to a realization that this is not for them. One afternoon, a firefighter was just going on ambulance duty when he heard a screech, a thud, and a hell of a lot of screaming.

A crowd gathered around an ice-cream truck that was parked just a hundred feet from his home. He ran over to see what the commotion was all about, and wondered if anyone needed assistance. By the time he got there, which was only a minute or two from the time he heard the noises, a siren was blaring and a cruiser was on its way.

All were huddled around a mother and father who were kneeling next to their son who was lying in the road. The police officer immediately called for the ambulance and within minutes, that was on its way. A young boy of about 8 or 10 years old ran out in front of the ice cream truck to cross the street. He didn't look for oncoming traffic, and he did not see the car coming along in the opposite direction. The driver of the car saw him but it was too late. He slammed on his brakes but was unable to stop before the vehicle ran into the young boy. The force of the vehicle knocked the youngster over, and the little guy was in serious trouble.

The firefighter and police officer were checking for injuries just as the ambulance pulled up. Care was taken not to cause any further injury and it was off to the emergency room with the child and his parents. The firefighter went back to his vehicle and drove to the station where he would be signing in on the roster for ambulance duty. By the looks of what he had witnessed, he felt that he would be going to the emergency room for a run that would take the youngster to a better-equipped facility in a larger hospital in the nearest city.

Sure enough, not even a half an hour into the shift, he was on his way to the emergency room. The doctor on call had treated the child as best he could and had him ready to go. A nurse was present in the "meat wagon," a term used by some for the ambulance, and was monitoring the IV drip and other vital signs while the firefighter simply sat back quietly, listened to the boy's moaning, and looked at his young but almost lifeless body.

He also listened to the parents in the front of the ambulance. They were talking and praying to God, just as if God was the ambulance driver. They made all kinds of deals with this God of theirs just to keep their son alive. The boy did make it to the hospital in the city and was alive when all left for home. However, the firefighter read the sad news in the paper a few days later that the young boy had died.

It really affected this firefighter, for he had youngsters at home close to that child's age. All he could see in his mind for several weeks was the little boy moaning in the back of the ambulance. And every so often, the boy took on the resemblance of his own two sons. This was not good. He thought about it long and hard. He had no problem seeing young men and women in accidents and witnessing the deaths of older people, but little kids did not sit right in his mind.

If there were going to be more of these types of calls, and there would be, ambulance duty would not be for him. 'Doc' just took away his own title and quit the ambulance squad. Firefighting would be okay, but not attending in an ambulance. Once his mind was made up, he informed the squad that he would help out in any other way with the organization, but he would never set foot in another ambulance again.

OF PRIESTS AND BROKEN LEGS

The fires of hell are here on earth. No one is immune from the ravages of fire, not even priests. Churches burn, and so do the dwelling places where holy men live. It was late evening when a box alarm was sounded for the Catholic Church located about a mile away from two station houses. It is ironic that even though some firefighters may not attend church, everyone seems to turn out for a church fire or rectory fire. There is something about these types of fires: many people feel as though they just should not happen.

Well, this night was not just any night. The box was pulled by a passerby, because he saw smoke and flames coming from the rectory across the street from the church. Once the alarm was sounded, almost every firefighter responded. Even though the response time was good, one of the priests living in the rectory on the second floor couldn't get out by the stairwells, but went out onto the second floor porch and tried to drop down to the ground. He was successful in escaping the fire, but was not so lucky otherwise, since he broke both of his legs when he landed.

The fire was stubborn, because it was an old-fashioned balloon-framed structure with additions and dropped ceilings scattered here and there. Interior and exterior attacks were in progress. Ladders were raised. Roofs were being vented. All was going as well as could be expected with full manpower and equipment. As an interior attack was being conducted up the front stairwell to the third floor and attic area, something happened that scared the living daylights out of the three men at the nozzle end.

DEACON TONY SUROZENSKI

31

An adjustable tip nozzle was being used effectively, being swirled around aimed at the cherry-red ceiling. The color was fading as the water hit it. Steam was all about the area from the intense heat. All of a sudden, the water flow stopped. The men, with a puzzled look on their faces, saw the ceiling turn the cherry-red that it was before, and pieces began to fall down. The nozzle was immediately dropped and all followed the hose line out of the building.

Once out, all seemed to yell simultaneously: "Who the hell shut the water off on us?" "Who was the stupid bastard that tried to kill us?" It turned out that one of the chiefs thought it best to get another gate on a hydrant so that more hose lines could be connected, thereby making short order of the fire.

However, the chief thought no one was in the building and that everyone had been told of his plan. Not so, not so. Poor communication left some stranded, but fortunately all escaped unharmed. Remember, not everyone had radios back then. Was this an excuse? No. But it did make it a little easier to understand.

The rectory was saved, but not to the point where it was feasible to remodel. A new one stands at the site of the old, with all the fire-safety features that it could have. As for the priest with the broken legs, he never seemed to get back to being his old self: his legs just didn't heal right. He suffered for a long time. It was, in a sense, a type of hell on earth for him. A fire has a way of doing that to a person, holy or not.

THIS PICTURE WAS TAKEN AS FLAMES BROKE THROUGH THE ROOF OF THE ST. LOUIS PARISH RECTORY SHORTLY BEFORE 1 A.M. SUNDAY

FIRE HAS NO RELIGIOUS PREFERENCE

COURTESY-WEBSTER TIMES

DEACON TONY SUROZENSKI

33

TRUSTWORTHY, MAYBE –
LONELY AND SCARY, DEFINITELY

On another warm night, a fire had struck a mansion-type home. The home was one where the stairwell reminded many of the film, "Gone with the Wind," because it wound down from the second floor and spread open into a huge foyer, leading to a very spacious living room, and a gigantic dining area, kitchen, and pantry.

A great deal of the structure had been destroyed by the fire: every room was charred, ceilings were down, and parts of the banister were no longer standing or secure. The dining room table and kitchen were covered with ceiling plaster. Firefighters cleared the areas all about the first and second floor to just waist width, leaving only a small inch-and-a-half hose line to dowse any hot spots that may flare up. Pockets of steam rose up here and there, and made the house look like the hot springs of the national parks.

The Fire Marshall had been called in to investigate the cause, but no serious overhauling was to be done until the owner's insurance claim adjuster was present to take pictures and file a claim. In order for this to take place, someone had to stand by and watch the place overnight. This someone, according to the insurance company, had to be trustworthy.

When the chief asked if a teacher/firefighter would do, the answer was in the affirmative, and so a particular firefighter was placed on night watch with only a hand radio and a hydrant wrench for protection. Protection from whom or what was the question. Who knew? The surrounding neighborhood was not what some would call problematic; however, one never knows who or what might show up once the fire was reported on the radio.

The job was fairly easy. All the firefighter had to do was walk around every fifteen minutes or so to make sure there were no hot spots, and to make sure no one was trying to break in to steal anything. Hot spots! No problem. But breaking and entering? Isn't that police duty? Well, all he had to do was get on the handheld radio and within minutes the police would be there. But minutes could be too late in certain circumstances. Those were thoughts that kept cropping up in the firefighter's mind.

Shortly after 2:00 A.M., as the watchman was making his rounds, he heard a groan, as if someone had fallen or bumped their head. He noticed that a window in a hallway which led to the kitchen was opened slightly, and on other passes he'd made that evening, he could have sworn that it was closed. This would be a good time to call for police assistance. Sure enough, within two to five minutes a cruiser was on scene, with two officers available to search the area. The firefighter went around with them. They all noticed that a box about the size of an apple crate was outside next to the opened window, but no other signs of entry into the building could be found.

The officers then made a thorough search inside and outside the premises and made sure the window was closed and secure. What a relief to the one on watch!

By 3:00A.M., another walk-through was made and all seemed well. No hot spots were noticed, and all one could hear was the water dripping and an occasional piece of ceiling falling to the floor below. Of course, the noises were quite exaggerated which made the firefighter's senses go to full alert, and his adrenaline and heart rate increased. All was in crisis mode, with the "fight or flight" mechanism in the brain ready to activate, with emphasis on the flight side.

Later, on another pass through the building, a voice of sorts was heard. Once again the radio was activated and police were there in minutes. This time the search revealed nothing except for a shoe print in the muddy area outside the house, which could have been there for some time and missed on the first pass. The officers said to the firefighter, "Don't hesitate to call at any time, even if we have to come here over and over again. It's better for us to do that than to have something happen to you." That was great reassurance, but it didn't eliminate his loneliness and fright each time the walk-through took place.

At about 4:30A.M., during another walk-through, the firefighter heard a loud groaning sound. This time, the "fight or flight" mechanism kicked in and the firefighter rushed through the doorway saying, "I'm leaving to go and sit in the pick-up truck. Take what you want. I don't care. They aren't paying me enough for you to cold-conk me."

He then left the building and sat in the pick-up truck that was left for him. Approximately ten minutes later, the firefighter heard the loud groan again; this time, however, he started laughing, and was embarrassed even though no one was there to see him. It turned out that the loud groaning was coming from an open window in a nursing home that was right across the street from the fire scene. 'Some old timer must have had a bad dream,' he thought. A sigh of relief was followed by a less frightening tour of the structure, one more time.

With no further chance of flare-ups, the firefighter went back to the truck to wait for the morning coffee and doughnuts that had been promised. When they finally arrived, he told the story to the men who brought the tasty breakfast. Somehow, the story got back to the chief. Being considered trustworthy is great, but being alone is not safe. From that day on, never again was one man left on night duty fire watch, alone.

MUTUAL AID – DUMB THINGS – EMBARRASING MOMENTS HEART ATTACK?

Call departments often rely on surrounding towns for assistance at fires, especially when it is difficult to get the manpower and apparatus at the scene. Many men and women in the firefighting service work outside of their respective towns during the day and it is often difficult to get even one truck on the road. Also, there are times when a structure fire demands all the help that can be mustered due to the size of the fire. And when weather conditions warrant the rotating of teams on a regular basis, it is good to have as many personnel on the scene as possible to get the job done. Hence, the need for mutual aid.

On one afternoon in late spring, a couple of decades ago, a neighboring town called for mutual aid to an old dairy plant. The brick and block structure was fully involved. The roof had fallen in at several places along the building, and flames licked out around the twisted metal and wooden beams.

The fire chief who was in command called for a ladder pipe to be set up near the back of the building. It was called for so that the fire could be attacked from a different angle. (For those who are not familiar with a ladder pipe setup, it is simply a large-diameter pipe that may be fitted with different sized nozzles, and which is attached to the end rungs of the ladder on a ladder truck. The pipe is kept on a stand near the back of the truck and is lifted on to the ladder after the ladder is extended a few feet. A handle is attached to the ladder pipe and a rope is attached to the handle so that it may be directed vertically from the base of the turntable. In some instances, it is tied off permanently so that a steady stream may flow in one area. This also gives a firefighter relief because they don't have to hold onto the rope for long periods of time.)

In any event, the truck, with its ladder pipe attached, was set up in the back of the building, as requested. However, before it was positioned, the driver noticed that there were power lines hanging in the way. If the ladder was set up above the power lines, the angle would not have been as advantageous as if it were set below them. The danger of setting the ladder below the power lines was quite apparent: if the electrical lines were to fall on the ladder, everyone associated with the truck could be electrocuted.

Immediately, the driver got on the radio to find out if the power had been cut to the lines going to the building. He received an answer that they were cut from the street so it was okay to extend the ladder. As it turned out, however, once the truck was set up, an assistant chief went by and gave the driver a hard time with all kind of expletives wanting to know who the stupid son of a bitch was who set up that way, and how dangerous it was to the driver and any firefighters who were on the ladder.

The assistant chief said that the lines were not cut from that side of the building but only from the main roadway. The electric company vehicle hadn't gotten to that utility pole yet. A lack of proper communications could have lead to death for some of the firefighters. Was someone up there watching over them?

Some may think that the lack of communication was the dumb thing and the embarrassing moment. Not so. All the firefighters knew that the seventy-five-foot ladder truck had a little problem with hydraulics due to its age: once the ladder was extended, it would slowly slide backward before it would lock in place. One had to be careful not to get a boot caught between the rungs as it slowly slid back.

The reader should now get the picture of an embarrassed firefighter whose foot was stuck between the rungs. Can one picture the firefighter moving this way and that and pulling on the boot to loosen it? How about the entire leg being pulled out of the boot and the one on the ladder tugging on the boot to free it? He finally climbed down the ladder and had the driver extend the ladder so that he could climb back up to get his boot back. One minor problem developed. Because the ladder was extended a bit too fast, the boot fell out and bounced off of the truck and into the rising water beneath it. One wet boot, one wet foot, and one red-faced guy waited for the ribbing of a lifetime back at the fire house.

The reader may think it was all over for the wet-footed firefighter. Well, it wasn't over yet. Because the ladder truck was set up in a low area, all the water from the various apparatus's discharges flowed into this low spot. The driver noticed that the water was rising up to the middle of the tire wells, which was not a good thing because there was much more water to flow into the area, and it could rise much higher, causing a problem with the electrical system. He also noticed that the flow from the ladder pipe was not doing anything significant to help extinguish the fire.

The driver asked for permission to move the vehicle and it was granted. Hoses were removed from the connections, the ladder pipe disconnected, and the truck was ready to be repositioned. The wet-footed firefighter began to pull on some of the two and a half inch diameter lines to get them out of the way. Fully charged lines under close to two feet of water is not an easy task. He was able to move one enough, though, so that the truck was able to maneuver properly. The wet-footed one was now a little wetter than before and felt like an adrenaline-filled weightlifter. This had proved to be more than he bargained for.

Back at the firehouse, the mundane task of unloading hoses, stacking them in the wash room, and re-packing the hose onto the trucks was in full swing. "Wet foot" began to notice some chest pains and slowed down quite a bit. He didn't say anything to anyone for fear of being ridiculed even more than before. He didn't want anyone to think that he was using that as an excuse to cover up the stupidity of the boot incident.

Finally, recall came in, the firefighters signed their rosters and all headed for home and a well-deserved rest. However, for "wet foot," the chest pains got worse. Fortunately, the hospital was on his way home, and as he tossed around the thought of going to the emergency room or not, the pain got so bad that he turned his vehicle into the driveway of the hospital, found a parking spot, and entered the emergency area. Now he was scared. He was only in his early thirties. He was too young to die. A prayer came to mind: "please help, I need you and my wife and kids need me to be around."

Once inside and his information given, he was immediately whisked into the emergency room, wired up, and given first-rate attention. Blood work indicated that something was going on but the monitors didn't show anything out of the ordinary. "It doesn't look like a heart attack but we will keep you overnight and monitor you to be sure." It was a great relief to hear those words. Further blood tests showed that nothing indicated a heart attack.

The doctors surmised that due to the extreme strain on the chest muscles while the firefighter was moving the hoses at the fire scene, he tore some muscles near the pericardial cavity which released substances into the bloodstream that gave them the suspicion of a heart problem. Once again, "wet foot" was relieved and said a silent prayer of thanks. He also enjoyed the attention of those who visited him that night and the next day. Did the ribbing stop? Hell, no. And that's one of the fun parts of being a firefighter. If you're not given a ribbing now and then, something must be wrong.

MUTUAL AID IS A GODSEND.
EXTRA ENGINES, LADDER TRUCKS, AND PERSONNEL
CAN MAKE A BIG DIFFERENCE

COURTESY OF THE WORCESTER TELEGRAM & GAZETTE

DEACON TONY SUROZENSKI

41

AN EXTERIOR ATTACH IS OFTEN NECESSARY
Courtesy of The Worcester Telegram & Gazette

DO AS I SAY, NOT AS I DO

Often, in a volunteer fire department, paid call, and the like, the Lieutenants and Captains and sometimes, the driver operators, plan training sessions whereby both officers and a driver may take groups of men and instruct them in proper firefighting techniques. One technique of breaking the window of a second-story dwelling using a "Pike Pole" was to stand off to the side of the window, and drive the tip of the pole, using an arcing motion, into the center of the window.

Normally, the glass will break and fall away from the firefighter, thus reducing the chance of getting injured by the falling glass. The pole may then be used to remove any remaining glass from the frame, or, if necessary, the curved end of the pole may be hooked over the center of the frame and pulled to remove the frame itself. Often this would be used on aluminum storm windows that covered the window that is part of the house. Once the glass was removed, a stream of water could be shot into the room or a ladder could be used to access the second floor. Additionally, a ladder could be extended to the side of the window and an ax could be used to remove the glass. These and many other methods are used, depending upon the circumstances of the structure fire. In any event, safety is always emphasized.

Not too long after that particular training exercise, a box alarm came in for a structure fire where a two-story building was involved, with smoke showing and flames coming out from under the eaves. As an engine company arrived, a full reverse was called for, because they came upon the structure that was involved in front of the hydrant that would supply water for the truck. It was also necessary to do so in order that the ladder truck, with its seventy-five foot extension ladder, could be positioned properly.

The second engine company then pulled up to the scene and tagged the hydrant that was closer to the structure fire. A hose company arrived shortly thereafter, and was positioned at an intersection where it could tap into a nearby hydrant that was located across from the fire. It was necessary to set up a thirty-five foot extension ladder at the rear of the building and men were attacking the fire from that position, as well as from the front, along with an interior attack which was advancing up a stairwell.

The ladder men were on the roof and were in the process of cutting a hole to vent the roof to release the buildup of dangerous smoke and gases. At one point, an officer called for a window to be knocked out in the middle of the second floor of the structure. A driver-operator, who heard the call, looked around, saw that his crew was all set, the truck was fine, and because no one else was available, ran to the ladder truck and removed a pike pole to use to break that window.

Since it was a hot day, and he'd been simply standing back by the truck, the driver didn't have his gloves on. Also, he didn't stand to the side, but proceeded to attack the window from an angle directly in front of him. Well, wouldn't you know, the window broke all right, and most of the glass hit his helmet and turnout gear so he was not hurt. However, one lousy piece of glass did not fall but slid down the pike pole and cut his middle finger right near the knuckle area.

One of the Assistant Chiefs noticed the incident, called for another driver to relive him, and immediately sent him over to the ambulance for some first-aid. While walking with him to the ambulance, he reamed him out for leaving his truck, no matter what the circumstances. "You can't do it all. You ain't "F'n Superman."

The first aid was fine to stop the bleeding but the driver had to be taken to the emergency room for stitches to the middle finger. Thoughts of what middle finger gestures imply entered his mind. Why that type of thought? The reader may have guessed. He would receive more ribbing from the guys, especially those of his own company who were recently trained by him.

By the way, this firefighter was none other than "wet foot." From that time on, and for quite some time thereafter, he was always asked if he could show them his $67.00 middle finger gesture. Why $67.00, one might ask? The firefighter had received that amount from the insurance company as compensation for his injury. Oh well, more ribbing was at hand, but at least he got some money for his troubles, and another good time was had by all.

PROPER POSITIONING OF A LADDER TRUCK IS IMPORTANT

Courtesy of The Worcester Telegram & Gazette

OF A HIGH SCHOOL FRIEND
AND THOSE BIG RED TRUCKS

How did it all begin for the $67.00 man? Back in the late fifties, "wet foot" and some of his friends were merely hanging around. Almost getting into trouble, as some teenagers can do, was just not cutting it. By trouble, the teen in question was one who hung around with guys who would like to experiment with drinking, either by taking some from their folks, or by trying to brew some of their own by allowing cider to harden. Some weekends of diarrhea were imminent, but they always seemed to blame it on bad food.

The saving grace came for the teen one evening when he went to a weekend dance. The guys gathered with their stash of booze and each had a sample slug before the dance. All seemed to be fine as they entered, but after a while, the heat inside seemed to get to them. The teen began to feel the room start to spin, and braced himself up against the wall.

Wouldn't you know, a police officer who was covering the dance walked right up to him and leaned against the wall just to his left shoulder? With a spinning head, the teen prayed to God as he never prayed before. The prayer went something like, "If I don't get caught, I promise that I will never drink again." Well, the police officer spoke to the teen: it was a normal sort of chit-chat, and the officer must have been satisfied that there was no problem, because he moved over to another part of the gym.

"Thank you, God" was the teen's response. However, he couldn't get over the fact that the cop seemed to be watching him no matter where he moved to. Slowly, the teen moved from that spot to a chair and then to another spot close to the door, always under the watchful eyes of that damned cop. Finally, he got outside and took off for home. He was lucky and made it home without incident.

Was he out of the woods yet? Nope. The spinning eased up but came back full force as soon as he got home. As quietly as he could, he snuck into the house and found that all had gone to bed. "Thank you, God," once again entered his mind. A mad but quiet dash to the bathroom left his stomach emptying into that porcelain bowl. While kneeling before it, he grasped the sides as he thought his entire intestines were going to end up in the toilet. "I never want to pray before that porcelain god again," entered his mind.

Now that he felt better, he began to move toward the hall which led to the stairwell which would have brought him to the safety of his room and the comfort of his bed. One minor problem arose: he could hear someone stirring from the room just above him. If it was his father, he was doomed forever.

Quickly, he moved back through the hall and into the den where he laid upon the sofa and began to pretend that he was asleep, all the while praying that same prayer, "If I don't get caught, I promise that I will never drink again."

A light switch went on and his dad passed through the den on his way to the bathroom. "Oh, please help me!" the drunken teen thought. "I wonder if I sprayed enough deodorizer to cover the lousy smell of vomit?" The sound of the toilet being flushed brought thoughts of being caught. Fear entered his system.

"Hey!" his father yelled as he entered the den. "I could smell vomit in the bathroom. What's going on?" "Crap." "Not enough spray." He thought that one more lie might just do the trick and so he responded with, "We went to get pizza and I ate way too much, and the orange soda with ice cream must not have agreed with me. That is why I am staying down here." And now for the old responsibility part, "I thought it best to do that so I wouldn't wake you and mom."

Well, it worked, but the sobering teen couldn't understand why he thought he heard his dad chuckling as he went back up to bed. Did he know? Did God tell him that he already learned his lesson? "Thank you, God." Would he honor his promise? Time would tell.

Shortly thereafter, one of his friends asked him if he would be interested in doing something worthwhile, like joining the Civil Defense Rescue Squad. His friend was quite the talker and had a gift for influencing people. He made being a member of the Rescue Squad quite exciting and also members were able to ride to fires on those big red trucks, a dream for many a young man since childhood. After some discussion with his parents about joining the Squad, all was set to launch the young adult onto a life of service to his community and beyond.

The leader of this Rescue unit had been appointed because of the skills he'd learned while in the armed services. He also learned much on his own, as well, as by attending training exercises offered by Civil Defense. This man ate, drank, and slept his vocation. He earned himself the nickname of "Rescue Eight," which was a television show about rescue within the fire services.

All who were members of the Squad were volunteers and were truly interested in serving the community in that capacity. Members learned all about first aid, knots and ropes and hitches for various rescue scenarios, lighting, generators, compressors, hydraulics, winches, pulleys, block and tackle, firefighting techniques, plus a host of other things related to safety and the emergency services.

He also was a paid call firefighter and a reserve police officer for the town. By some, he was looked upon as an oddball, but by others, he was looked upon as a hero. In any event, he was always available and always got the job done.

It was through his tutelage that the young adult got some valuable basic training in rescue and firefighting techniques and was forever grateful for it. He always showed that man honor and respect even when others teased the heck out of the Rescue Chief. The only time that the young adult felt uncomfortable around the Rescue Chief was the day that he had to tell him that he would no longer be a member of the Squad. This came about because leadership in the fire department had been watching the growth of the young adult and wanted him to move over to become a regular member of the paid call department.

The day came and sure enough, the CD leader was upset because he thought that the young man would become his right hand in the near future. In a sense, it did boil down to a money issue because the young adult was now about to get married and could use the extra money as he began to raise a family. And, who knew, according to his way of thinking, maybe he would someday become a firefighter in a full-time department. The move proved to be helpful in many ways, the least of which was, however, financial or towards membership in a full-time department.

The young adult grew into an adult, whatever that means, and did choose a career. The career was in the teaching profession, but he had the best of both worlds, because he could also be a firefighter and ride on one of those big red trucks.

CARMARADERIE AND THE BROTHERHOOD

One of the great things about firefighters is the gathering like family. Husbands and wives always got together on a regular basis at backyard parties in small settings and in larger ones such as a firefighters' ball. In a small town, people seem to know each other to some extent, but being attached to the fire service was and still is really special. It is like a brotherhood where everyone looks out for each other. At least that's the way it was for the teacher/firefighter.

He remembered that many a Fourth of July celebration involved families of firefighters enjoying each other's company. Birthday celebrations and wedding anniversaries were also in the mix for husbands and wives involved in the department. Almost every wife was a member of the Ladies Auxiliary. These ladies not only were instrumental in taking care of various events, but they were always a great asset at fires by supplying the weary firefighters with food and drink. They came out on the hottest days and on the coldest nights and never cared about not getting paid. Their loved ones were on the line and they wanted to be there for them in any way they could. Hot soups, coffee, sandwiches, doughnuts, burgers, water, and soft drinks were always welcome sights but never welcomed as much as those who delivered them.

Firefighters' wives make a lot of sacrifices, especially when it comes to anxieties brought about by the nature of the job. They don't know whether their husband will be back or not after he leaves home. "Keep him safe," is a prayer said by many a firefighter's spouse. The wives of Call and Volunteer Firefighters have the additional sacrifice of not having their husbands around during special events such as a child's birthday party, going out for dinner, a family gathering. They may start with their husbands present but when that alarm blows or the scanner goes off, the ladies understand that their affairs must be placed on a back burner and that there is someone in serious trouble who needs the assistance of their firefighter husband. The job involves saving lives and property and always giving to others at the expense of their own.

What they married into was a continual sacrifice of lack of presence at certain times. There are times when their lives are lonely and very scary. A prayer of many firefighters was, and still is "Keep my wife and family safe."

The experiences of the wife of the teacher/ firefighter seemed to be preparing her for something else in life. What it was did not become apparent for at least twenty years. It involved firefighting, the lack of her husband's presence, and much more. Prayers got her through many things in life and she would find that prayers would still be involved during her husband's future.

DRINKING AND FIREFIGHTING MIX —
WHAT A FINE MIX!

Is it tradition? Is it just one of those things that firefighters do well? Or is it part of the trade? All of the noted questions are about the consumption of alcohol. It appeared to the teacher/firefighter that all the men at the firehouse could really hold their liquor. It was nothing to get out of work, go down to the local gin mill, and down several beers with your firefighting buddies. Conversations would cover a variety of topics from home life and work, to movies and television programs, to sports and hobbies, and sometimes even topics about religion, and, of course, the last fire or two, or three, or of years ago.

Oh, those draft brews tasted so great and went down ever so smoothly, always loosening the tongue in an ever-so-relaxing manner.

Once in a while, a strange phenomenon occurred. No matter how lightheaded or numb feeling in the lips one may have experienced, when the fire alarm bellowed its beckoning call to report to the station, the firefighter's body had a way of pumping out adrenaline and other substances that would immediately place the person in sober mode. Or, at least it appeared to be so.

No one ever seemed to cause any problems in the area of drunk driving, nor of placing anyone in danger. The trucks were manned. The fires were attacked and put out. The trucks returned undamaged. Equipment was all checked, back in order, and hoses were set, ready for cleaning. This was often followed, depending upon the time of day, by a trip back to the watering hole to quench one's thirst with another foamy brew. This time the discussion was usually centered on

DEACON TONY SUROZENSKI

53

the incident that all just experienced. Positive and negative critiques were part of the talks, along with who did well and who "screwed up." Some fun-poking was a must, and for those who really did badly, the word crucifixion would be appropriate.

Often, when the fires involved serious traumatic incidents such as injury or loss of life, the bending of the elbow exercise and the conversation about the incident seemed to be quite therapeutic. Some might call it an old-fashioned type of Critical Incident Stress Management. Little did anyone realize that it was the conversation aspect that was the most therapeutic.

For those guys who really boozed it up to the point of being tipsy, if they didn't know enough to stay put, the others made sure that they never got off the bar stool. Designated drivers, they were not. Designated guardians of the leftover drinks, they were. Deep inside their inner cores, they were embarrassed by their lack of control and inability to serve in the manner in which they were accustomed to. But never would they admit it. Nor did anyone push the issue with them. They were firefighters and they paid their dues in the past. They were heroes who at that particular time just went a bit overboard with the booze and couldn't get on the big red truck at that moment. Hell, they couldn't even drive or walk to the station to get on one.

Fortunately for all concerned, no one ever got seriously hurt as a result of having had too much alcohol to drink, not in the town of the teacher/firefighter anyway. This would appear to be strange with the volunteer/call department because firefighters could be at home, relaxing after having a few drinks and an alarm could come in.

If a firefighter had a few drinks spaced out over a period of time, there wouldn't be much of an effect on his system but there could be an odor of alcohol on his breath. However, if there was too much alcohol in the system, that person could be racing to a fire, feeling quite sober, but in reality, would be considered under the influence by modern standards. The smart ones knew enough to stay home. The less intelligent were simply lucky.

Drinking and driving never mixed. Drinking and firefighting was always and still is a deadly mix. And yet, the drinking goes on. Fortunately, more firefighters are aware of the dangers and of the fact that DUI's do not cut it with family, friends, and careers. Smart officers pick up on problem drinkers and do their best to keep them off the trucks. With repeat offenders, the order of the day could lead to interventions: let the excessive problem drinker beware.

Some folks are slow learners, as it was with good old "wet foot." He started sneaking booze from his folks when he was a junior in high school. He and one of his cousins would occasionally sneak down into his parents' cellar and tap the gallon jug of a great tasting Concord grape homemade wine. Grandma had a way with that stuff. He was smart enough not to get caught because he always took a jug from the back of the shelf in the old wooden closet style chest. When the wine got down close to one half of the jug, all that was needed was to fill it back up with water. Who would know? This was done to several jugs over the years and no one ever seemed to get to those on the back shelf. He was safe as to no one finding out and he getting into trouble. So he believed and it so it came to pass.

Not much went on in the way of drinking while he was in college, but there were those occasional weekends away from home and family where a few beers were tipped and an occasional shot or two were slugged down. However, on his twenty-first birthday, he began a drinking spree that lasted for close to thirty years. Why, he was so good at holding his liquor that when his first son was born, he celebrated with a few of the guys at the barroom that was located within a twenty-foot walking distance from the firehouse. Now, how wonderful was that?

He could hold his liquor so well that he was able to down twenty shots of ginger brandy and twenty four glasses of beer in approximately two hours and drive a drunk home. And the drunk wasn't him. In reality, he was under the influence, but it didn't kick in until he got home. Fortunately for him, he made it without incident. However he did pray in front of the oval porcelain altar of Bacchus and eject all the contents of his stomach into that bowl. Drinking a whole bottle of pink medicine helped him to soothe his stomach, but it never helped to stop the room from spinning. Even one foot placed hard onto the floor wouldn't stop the spin. After a few more trips to the oval bowl and prayers of promise never to drink again were offered, he finally was able to get to sleep.

DEACON TONY SUROZENSKI

The next morning was not great at all. The firefighter/teacher, old "wet foot" (of course this was well before he took on that name) was quite pale and shaky. Too bad he had contracted to help his friend break up an old concrete walk that morning. A weak and shaky firefighter/teacher had to live up to his promises, and so he swung a twenty pound sledgehammer onto the concrete. "Bang." "Bang." "Bang." The sounds echoed in his head ever so loudly.

He could hardly lift up the hammer after about only an hour of work. Boy, pounding down the drinks was a lot easier than pounding down the sledgehammer. And then there was the picking up of chunks of concrete and placing them in the wheel barrow, and pushing the wheelbarrow all the way up a plank and onto a dump truck.

The push up the ramp seemed a lot tougher than carrying a hose-pack up a thirty-five foot ladder. Oh, the ejection of unwanted stomach contents took place in the dump truck after each load was emptied into the truck. The owner of the property commented to the boss that it didn't look as though that young man was cut out for that type of work.

If only she knew how embarrassed he was due to excessive drinking, she would have understood the situation a lot better. Fortunately, the intoxicated, hung-over worker only had to be there for the morning. Noon couldn't have come fast enough. Water was a real friend even though it seemed to have a sickening effect on his system.

By the time the proud, hung-over father got to the hospital to see his wife and newborn son, his bodily system began to adjust and return to a somewhat normal state. This did not stop the smell of alcohol emanating from his body and breath. His wife did not appreciate that type of cologne or the fact that the alcohol produced it, and she sent him home after a short while.

What luck, as the dizzy, insensitive, selfish lug needed to sleep. And that he did. His flowers and gift at the evening visit were more in tune with what was right and proper. Thank God for a forgiving wife. The future would echo that statement many times over. He was a slow learner.

FUN AND GAMES – THE MUSTERS AND MORE DRINKING OPPORTUNITIES

Promises are often hard to keep, even if they are made to God. How would it be for a healthy, macho young firefighter not to be able to show how much booze he could handle without getting drunk, especially after his drinking escapade when his son was born? God would understand.

Of course, the young firefighter would have to use every trick in the book to keep himself from overdoing it. A thing like drinking a bottle of pink bismuth liquid before going out to an event where drinking would be involved was one of them. Another was to be sure he had a lot of milk and food before he went out. All of those sure did the trick, most of the time.

One of the best opportunities to have a great drinking time was after an event called the "Fireman's Muster." This was a really fun time where families and friends attended and cheered their local department on during the various events. One simple event involved the connecting of several lengths of hose line, attaching a nozzle to the end, turning on the water, and then hitting a target with the water stream from the nozzle.

Another was the bed race where the firefighter's gear was set beside a cot. Four men were involved. When the sound was struck for the start, the men would get up from the cot, put on all of their gear, and race to connect the lines and hit a target with the stream of water coming from the hose. All was a race against time, and the fastest time won the prize. Sometimes it was hilarious, especially when the connections were not threaded properly and the water sprayed all over the contestants. Even funnier was watching some guys getting dressed and trying to run, only to realize that the gear was not on properly. A few looked like old-timers trying to run while tugging on their suspenders. "Drag a leg. Pull on the suspenders. Hop a few steps. Drag a leg. Pull on the suspenders."

All this was in operation while trying to get to the hose couplings and nozzle. Once in a while, the hydrant man would not get his gate on properly and he would get soaked. Laughter sounded out all over the place along with good hearted jeers such as, "What's a matter boy couldn't hold it? Wet your pants did ya?" It truly was a fun time.

After the musters was a time for good food and good cheer. Pitchers of foamy beer slid around many tables. If one were not careful, it was easy to overdo it. Thank God for the pink stuff and a lot of food. Just a little buzz triggered the warning to stop if you wanted to get back to the station safely and avoid some choice words from a loving, concerned wife.

But then there was that one time when just one more led to two and three and more, and "honey" needs to drive home. More promises were made. More promises were broken. Thank God for forgiving wives and, of course, a forgiving God. How long could this go on?

THE FIREFIGHTER FINDS RELIGION
IS IT ALL OVER AS A FIREFIGHTER?

During those drinking years and good times at musters and at the annual Firefighter's Ball, the young man began to do some serious thinking about his life and where it might leave him. Could he do this stuff forever? Firefighting was very rewarding and the friendships and brotherhood were fantastic. The bending of elbows was simply great, but could it last?

He was getting older and involved in just about everything one could think of in school and community besides being a firefighter. He was vice president of the local Boy's Club, was vice president of the teacher's union, chaired a number of school-related committees, chaired a school building committee, was appointed Communications Officer for the Fire Department and later became Captain of Ladder One.

However, there still seemed to be something missing in his life. His family was growing older with two kids in junior high school and one in elementary school. Just what was missing? Could it be that there was one aspect of the wholeness of body, mind, and spirit that was missing? Could it be that spiritual side?

Being a good "Catholic boy," he did attend Mass every weekend. However, he often wondered that if it were not for his wife, would he miss on occasion or even bother to go at all? There were those times when he sat in church thinking about how he was going to build his house. And there were those times when he was relieved when the fire alarm blew during the Mass and he was able to skip out. It was legal in his eyes to do so. Helping someone in trouble was more important than just sitting there. One could be saving a life, and that was a good thing. But was he being called to something else?

He was reminded of the time when his son was in the hospital at only eighteen months old and the prognosis did not look good for his recovery. He had promised God that if he would heal his son, he would drive his mother and her friend to their favorite novena to St. Jude, which was in a church several miles out of town. He remembered that the doctor told him and his wife to go home and get some rest and that he would call them if the situation got worse. The firefighter/ teacher made the promise on his way out to the car and when they got home, they received a phone call from the doctor to come pick up their son because the fever broke and there were no signs of any illness whatsoever. It appeared to be a miracle because the doctor couldn't explain the change that took place so quickly. One minute it looked as if there was no hope for the little guy and the next, the signs were gone and he was in perfect health.

Well, unlike the promise not to drink, this was one he had to keep and he did. It turned out that he not only drove them to the novena, he went inside and participated, and liked it. His own prayer was for him to be the best at whatever God wanted of him. Little did he know at the time that his mother and wife were praying for the same thing. Many years went by and a few voluntary drives to the novenas most likely led to the firefighter's questioning and a call to return to a deeper faith. But what would the guys think of this twist of fate for the (self proclaimed) macho firefighter?

What is one to think if in reality the call to a deeper faith is present? If one is open to the call, and it is a true calling, everything else will somehow fall into place. The events and situations for growth will be presented and growth will take place. And so it did for the firefighter/teacher.

One Sunday, just before Mass ended, there was a call from the altar for help in the area of religious education. They were looking for teachers, and he wondered if this was what he was being called to. Not being quite sure if he was ready for this, the firefighter thought that if he put off calling the rectory long enough, they would have all the help they would need and he would be free to continue just as he was for the time being.

CALLED TO SERVE

Well, wouldn't you know, he phoned the priest and was told that all the slots were filled but that he would keep him on the substitute list in the event a teacher were to call in sick. This was fine, and so he thought that he was off the hook, and that it didn't look like this was what he was being called to do. This proved to be incorrect when he received a call from the priest wanting to know if he was still interested in teaching, because one of his teacher's parents was ill and that teacher was not able to continue. He sure couldn't say no at that point if his word meant anything.

So, the "yes" to that priest led to teaching what was then called "CCD" or Confraternity of Christian Doctrine. The extra training that was involved lead to certification as a master catechist with a concentration in youth ministry. Ah. This must have been what he was being called to. Time proved that it was only a step to something else within the Catholic Church.

The firefighter/CCD teacher was now involved in youth ministry, which led him to the experience of working on retreats for teens. The name of the retreat style was Teens Encounter Christ or TEC retreats. While on one of those retreats, he met a couple of young gentlemen who were also part of the retreat team. These two young men, who were in their late teens, appeared to be quite religious and spiritual in their own right. One evening, after all the scheduled programs were over, they invited the firefighter to a prayer service, and wondered if he was ever prayed over before. He said that he hadn't and thought that it would be interesting.

The chapel where the prayer service was to be held was set up in a monastic style, with seats and kneelers on both sides of the chapel, facing each other. The center was open, and the aisle led to an altar that was on a slightly raised platform. On the wall behind the altar was a huge crucifix. The vertical part of the cross was about twelve feet high and the horizontal span was around eight feet in length. A light was focused on the crucifix which made the body look life-like. A really neat feature of the entire chapel was the fact that the floors were heated.

This was quite appealing to the man who was taking part in the service because he often said that he did most of his best thinking while in a horizontal position, on his back, with his feet slightly raised. So

DEACON TONY SUROZENSKI
61

he asked the two young men if it would be all right to lie right in front of the altar, facing the crucifix with his feet resting on the platform that supported the altar. They thought that it was a bit unorthodox, but they both agreed to it. A small pillow was made available for his head and he took the new prayer position.

The two men positioned themselves by kneeling just behind the very comfortable-looking person who was lying on the floor and began to pray the Lord's Prayer. Then one of the guys produced some holy oil and made the sign of the cross on the comfortable one's forehead. Then they both extended their hands over him in prayer. At first it was silent but then strange words started coming from one of the guy's mouths. It almost sounded like the Polish language with the 'sh' and 'ch' sounding words; however, he was of Polish descent, and understood a little of the Polish language. This was not Polish.

While all this was going on, the CCD teacher was staring at the corpus of Jesus that was on the cross and felt a tingling sensation throughout his head. He then thought that these two guys were nuts and he wanted to get out, but for some reason he could not move. Now, he was a bit scared for this was something that he had never experienced in his entire life.

While he was experiencing the strange tongues, the tingling sensation, and inability to move, as soon as the young man who was praying switched his prayer to the "Hail Mary," all sensations stopped. The man on the floor, still focusing on the crucifix throughout all of this, immediately felt an extreme sense of peace, and while relaxing his arms out to his side to parallel the outstretched arms of Jesus, he silently said in his mind, "whatever you want me to do, I will do it. I am yours."

That began a chain of events that led him on an adventure that he would cherish for the rest of his life. And the adventure would include the fire services.

WHAT THE HECK IS A DEACON ANYWAY?

The next morning brought an interesting thought to the firefighter/teacher who had this "religious experience." On his way down to breakfast, he noticed a poster on one of the walls in the hallway that said, "Ever think of becoming a deacon?" He hadn't noticed that before. And he had been to that retreat place a few times before within the past month. He also noticed the same poster in the cafeteria and another on the way out of the building. A deacon, he thought? What the heck is that all about? Was this simply a coincidence or was this the beginning of a call to the order of deacon in the Catholic Church? Time would tell.

After the TEC (Teens Encounter Christ) retreat was over, he still felt a bit strange and at peace. This sense of peace was like nothing he had ever experienced before. He also had what seemed to be a constant urge to pray. He had been given a pair of rosary beads on the retreat so he began to pray the rosary. The Joyful Mysteries popped into his mind. He started out with the "Apostles' Creed," then on the large bead next to it he prayed the "Lord's Prayer." This was followed by the "Hail Mary" on three consecutive beads, then a "Glory be to the Father, and to the Son and to the Holy Spirit." Now began the first mystery, called the "Annunciation," where the angel Gabriel announced that Mary was chosen to be the mother of Jesus, The Christ, The Son of God. The "Lord's Prayer" was prayed on the large bead and this was followed by the "Hail Mary" which was said on the ten beads following the large one. At the end was the "Glory be" again, and the next mystery was meditated upon.

DEACON TONY SUROZENSKI

The other mysteries, biblical in reference, were "The Visitation," where Mary visited her kinswoman, Elizabeth. "The Birth" of Jesus was next. "The Presentation of Jesus in the Temple" was after that, and finally, the last mystery to be meditated upon was "Finding Jesus in the Temple." It took all of about twenty-five minutes to pray the rosary which was just about the same amount of time it took to get home from the retreat house. It truly was a relaxing drive home. What a beautiful way to spend a commute. One could be relaxed, alert, and praying at the same time.

When he did get home he realized that he was still under the influence of that strange experience and seemed to be full of peace and love. When he got home, he hugged his wife and kids and began to talk about the wonderful time he had had that weekend. However, wouldn't you know, there was a "Wait till your father gets home" situation on the horizon. His darling wife reminded him that he was back from the mountaintop experience and into reality. Report cards needed to be looked at and signed and by the tone of her voice, she was not too pleased with some of the children's grades.

Well, when Dad asked to see them, they were literally shaking in their boots. However, to their surprise, all he said was, "I am really disappointed in you two. If you don't get these grades up, you will never get to do the things that you really want to do in life. What do you think a good disciplinary measure might be to assist you in bringing those grades up?" Wow, they thought. What is going on here? Usually he rants and raves and whacks us on our rear ends and grounds us for months. What happened to him? So they responded with, "Gee Dad, you should go on these retreats more often." Dad simply laughed and continued to focus on what they would do to bring those grades up. Extra study time was what all agreed upon. Some of the grades did go up markedly and others just slightly, but they did go up and all were pleased with the results.

So how long did the peaceful experience last? It lasted for months and into years, but it was like a yo-yo with ups and downs. There were more strange experiences and downright dull nothingness. Throughout all of the time, though, the thought of the poster about becoming a deacon kept on surfacing. What the heck is a deacon, anyway?

DEACON TONY **SUROZENSKI**

65

IS HE LOSING HIS MIND OR WHAT?

Good old Dad was slowly getting back to normal as far as the usual routine of home life was concerned. Grass got cut. Some reading and studying took place. Dishes and household chores were shared with an occasional raised voice when the kids didn't react in the time frame that Dad thought they should. The fire scanner would go off from time to time and the mad dash for the coat, hat, and race to the car took place. The red light would flash with its pulsating rhythm as the car sped off down the road to the fire station. An occasional mumble of not too nice comments would surface when the car's horn was blown and the car in front wouldn't pull over. "Freaking idiots." "What if it was their house on fire?" "Pull over, you stupid idiot." Yes, back to normal it was, at least to some degree anyway.

A few things changed somewhat, like the lack of the use of a four letter word that began with the letter "F." Gone was any use of the name of Jesus Christ other than in the context of a reference to religion or the Gospels. Even the phrase, "Oh my God" was now non-existent. Now, time was set aside for prayer, and not just the usual morning or evening prayer that took about twenty seconds to say. There was a good half hour to an hour of prayer time. Sometimes there was even music in the background.

However, this additional prayer time brought on some questionable experiences that made good old Dad question his sanity. Because he taught the sciences, it seemed to be part of his nature to question everything and try to find an explanation for whatever he experienced. But sometimes there just didn't seem be any logical explanation that could be proven. How could he explain the smell of roses in the house while praying when there were no roses in the house, nor was his wife using any rose-scented perfume, no candles or bathroom sprays, and no candies or anything that would give off the odor of roses could be found in the house? He even went outside to find out if there was anything out there even though it was mid-winter. Strange was the only word that came to mind.

Another mind-boggling event took place once when he was lying on the couch while looking up at a picture of Jesus. The shoulders were covered with a white ruffled material that resembled a tunic. The face was of a color that would be typical of a man of Mediterranean descent. This Jesus had darker hair and brown eyes. The eyes were situated such that they would seem to penetrate the one who was gazing upon them and would seem to follow the person if that person moved to the right or to the left. Religious music was playing in the background. When the song with the lyrics, "Here I am, Lord. Is it I, Lord? I have heard you calling in the night," came up, the face and head appeared to change from the original to different faces with different hair styles.

This happened twelve different times during that single gaze. What is going on, he thought: Am I going crazy or what? Blinking didn't change anything; turning away and then back didn't either. He even thought it might be the devil playing tricks on him. A bit of fear crept in but was eased when another song began to play, "Be not afraid, I go before you. Come, follow me, and I will give you rest." Wow. He thought it would be in his best interest to call his pastor and to make an appointment to see him to discuss these strange phenomena.

The phone call and appointment were made. The pastor listened intently and told him that he would set up an appointment with a priest who was much more knowledgeable than he about these types of experiences. During that visit, the bewildered firefighter/teacher was told that these things do happen and not to worry about losing it or being crazy. The words of wisdom, to accept it for what it might be, a courting period with God because he may be calling you seemed to be quite logical. The priest said that if it was of God, that he would be led in the right direction and be at peace with the decision. And so, it was left at that. The face changes in the picture stopped. The scent of roses continued off and on for a while. The sense of peace continued along with the thought of becoming a deacon. So, what does one do about that?

ASK A DEACON AND DON'T FORGET YOUR WIFE

The simple answer was to ask another deacon about his calling, and this is exactly what he did. He also talked with his wife about it at length. She was not in favor of him becoming a deacon. She already was a 'firefighter's widow" because he was gone quite often. This would just add fuel to the fire of loneliness and who knew what that could lead to? It wasn't until they both visited a deacon and his wife that she began to put her mind at ease and pray about his request.

There was a new class opening for diaconate studies and he was wondering if he should apply. He also prayed about it. The call was quite strong. The thought of being a deacon was constantly on his mind. But he knew that if his wife would not consent, it just wouldn't happen.

One day, while shooting the breeze with the guys after a practice at the fire station, his wife came in, out of the blue, and said, with a tear in her eye and a smile on her face, "How do you fight God? If you want to be a deacon, go ahead and apply." The look of shock on his face and the tears that fell from his eyes clinched it. He hugged her and left with her to discuss her change of heart.

This change of heart came about because of an inexplicable experience that she had had while praying about the diaconate in church. She was kneeling in a pew about midway down the aisle. She was facing the Tabernacle where the reserved Eucharist was kept, and kept glancing up at the large crucifix that hung just above the altar. It was about the same size as the one her husband had gazed upon at the retreat. Suffering and sacrifice came to mind as she looked upon it and again looked back at the Tabernacle.

Then, out of the clear blue, came the scent of roses. She wondered about that. However, there was no one in church and the windows were closed. No fans or circulators were on. When she thought about the diaconate, the scent seemed to surround her and she began to feel at peace. "Ok," she said, "If this is what you want for us, then he can become a deacon." The scent then got stronger and faded as she felt a deep sense of peace envelop her.

As she related the story to her husband, they both felt a sense of peace and prayed for the strength to enter this new adventure with God. The application went in the mail the very next day. He was received into the program and was ordained a deacon four years later. But, what about the fire department?

DIACONATE FORMATION AND SACRIFICES

The diaconate formation period of approximately four-and-a-half years from the time of application to the ordination date didn't change things at the fire department for this soon-to-be deacon. He now was a captain of a ladder company, and even though the preparation time of two nights a week for three hours per night was somewhat taxing, the teacher/firefighter somehow managed to develop training sessions, run the company, and fight fires.

However, he did begin to feel the stress of this difficult balancing act and knew that something had to go. He still loved fishing, hunting, and an occasional game of golf, but he noticed that he wasn't getting the same enjoyment out of any of them like he did in the past. All of that went by the wayside, and was replaced with spending time on diaconal studies.

Of course, one couldn't forget the family and work aspect. And guess what? He came to the conclusion that the Church did not need a scandal so he gave up drinking. He felt that the Church didn't need a drunken deacon who would be the talk of the town if he ever got into an accident or said something ridiculous while under the influence of alcohol. This was no easy task for a man who was able to drink a bottle of Scotch, or two, in the course of an afternoon and evening.

He came to this conclusion while he was teaching a high school class about alcohol addiction and twelve-step programs including AA, Alcoholics Anonymous. He was going over a checklist of symptoms and recognized that he was checking off almost all of them for himself, including one about blacking out and not remembering an event. How could one forget, especially a New Englander, that he ate steamed clams at a dinner at Cape Cod with some good friends?

He remembered another incident when he had too much to drink, still felt that he was sober enough to drive his big eight-cylinder Cougar, saw two double solid lines in the road and decided to follow the two that were in the middle, but just missed hitting a utility pole on the side of the road. If he had hit it, he could have killed his wife. Those two particular incidents kept haunting him: especially the one about almost killing his wife. It was time he practiced what he preached about the dangers of alcohol and time to "Do as I do, as well as what I say."

His help came from some of his friends that he met in church every day. They were in AA and had already realized that they could not succeed without the help of a higher power. They were in church daily as part of their recovery process and would talk to their friend, the teacher, the firefighter, the soon to become deacon, about AA. Once he realized that he had a problem and declared it to be true, he was on his way to recovery. One thing blocked him from doing the AA thing, however. He did not think that he had the time to go to meetings with his schedule.

One day, while praying, he asked his Higher Power, in his case, Jesus, to help him overcome the drinking problem without going to meetings. He never did go to any and remained alcohol-free for fourteen years. He didn't realize until later on that his morning sessions with his AA buddies after Mass were like attending mini-meetings. So in reality, he was helped by those guys and by the grace of God. When he looked back upon those sessions he felt that those men were filled with Christ and were acting like the good Christians that they were baptized to be.

With all those sacrifices made, it was time for one more, and this one was the big one, the fire department. The candidate for the diaconate came to realize that if he were to do ministry effectively, firefighting effectively, and teaching effectively, and most importantly, remain faithful to his vocation of matrimony, something had to go. His wife and children were certainly not going, his teaching position brought in the money to support the family, and now, a ministry was soon to be in place. Only one thing was left. The old saying of "You can't have your cake and eat it, too" seemed to apply here.

After much thought and prayer, he told his wife that he was quitting the fire department and that he would draft a letter just prior to ordination. She was quite relieved.

The teacher/firefighter was ordained in April of 1990 and began his ministry in a nearby town which was only a twenty to thirty minute drive from his home. As a deacon, it was agreed that he would minister in the parish for twelve to fifteen hours per week. This included his weekend Masses along with the time spent in his primary ministry of preparing families for their children's baptisms. It was quite fulfilling and he visited ninety eight families that first year. Needless to report, it took more than fifteen hours per week to visit those families and minister in other ways within the parish.

This proved, and gave him some sense of comfort, that he had made the right decision to leave the fire department. So, was it all over for him, as far as the fire department was concerned? Well, the reader may wish to know that once his letter of resignation was submitted, the Chief of the department said that he did not want to lose him. The Chief, asked him that when he was ordained, would he like to be the Fire Chaplain for the Department? What do you think the answer was?

NOW THE DEACON/CHAPLAIN

That June, the fire department had a new Chaplain, and the ties were never broken. Was that part of God's plan? Time would tell. The newly-ordained deacon was thrilled to be part of the Department in his new capacity as Chaplain. He never lost his rank of Captain. The Chaplain would visit the firehouse on his free time on Saturdays and once in a while during the week. He attended the Firefighter's Ball, where he gave the blessing before the meal. He was present for retirement dinners and special events. And every year he gave the opening prayer on Firefighter's Sunday and then served at Mass where the firefighters gathered to remember those who had gone before them. He also preached at those Masses and was even ribbed there, before the Mass began, and was told to keep his homily short because breakfast was waiting at a nearby restaurant. Ah. Once again, he was one of them. It's all in the ribbing.

Some of the less pleasant duties were encountered when members of the fire department or their families died. Those were difficult times because nothing can be fixed. You aren't Jesus. You can't raise someone from the dead. Comfort by presence is about all one can bring to families during those trying times. What does one say to those who know that their loved one is not coming back? All the wrong things pop into a chaplain's mind, such as "Oh, he lived a good life, so we know he is in heaven;" or "He is in a better place now, free from pain." No way should anyone say that to a family member, even if those responses are believed to be true. They do not take the pain away, and the families would rather have their loved one with them, alive. So, a loving, caring, presence does more good than words. In the chaplain's mind, when it came to times like these, it was a lot easier to be in a burning building putting the "wet stuff on the red stuff."

As time moved on, there was more of the same old thing with regard to the chaplaincy. Dinners, special occasions, retirement parties and the like were getting to be old hat. There was very little excitement in being a "banquet chaplain." Wasn't there more that he could do?

Photo by Alan J Brackett

A TIME TO RELAX, PRAY, AND REMEMBER

Firefighter Sunday - Webster, Massachusettes

FROM BANQUET CHAPLAIN TO THE FRONT LINE

One early December evening, the chaplain was heading to a health clinic in the nearby city to try to get some relief from intense pain that was coming from the area near his right ear. When he got closer to the main thoroughfare, he noticed that the traffic was slowing down and that there was a big glow in the sky. As he got closer, the traffic was detoured off the highway because flames and smoke were pouring out from the top and sides of a large storage building that was adjacent to the highway. He thought, "Boy, they sure have their hands full. It must be a multi-alarm assignment with mutual aid from the nearby towns."

Little did he realize that six firefighters were going to be trapped and die in that building. He switched his radio to a local news channel and got a better idea of what was going on. When he finally got into the clinic, he mentioned to the receptionist that there was a huge fire in the city. She switched the television on and was able to catch news clips of the fire. Notification of possible loss of firefighters was then reported. The chaplain prayed for all concerned and was in no condition to get to the scene, although he really wanted to see if there was anything that he could do to help. His ear and throat hurt so much that he decided that it would be best to get home.

The next morning, as soon as he woke up, the chaplain turned the television on to get the latest about the fire. He witnessed a female fire chaplain being interviewed. "A female chaplain?" he thought. That was a switch for him. "And she was on the scene helping out and mentioning that other chaplains were there assigned to families who lost their loved ones in the fire." He wanted to get right out there, but due to the fever, dizziness, and pain, he would have to wait. Finally, after a few days, he was able to get to the scene because the firefighters were still searching for the bodies. The chaplain felt strange walking to the scene with a jacket and a hard hat while all the other chaplains had white helmets and turnout gear.

This caught the attention of one of the other chaplains. He asked if he was a chaplain and that if he ever heard of the Massachusetts Corps of Fire Chaplains. The hard hat chaplain said yes to the first part of the question and no to the second part. The fully-geared chaplain introduced himself as a deacon from Salem, and when he found out that the guy he was talking to was also a deacon, he asked if he would like to become a member of the Corps, and if he would like to get an ID badge so that he could assist at the scene. The other deacon/chaplain answered yes and was soon assisting on the scene.

He was introduced to another deacon/chaplain from Northborough. Both discussed how they were sick of simply being "banquet chaplains" and were thinking about resigning their chaplaincy positions. However, both agreed to give this MCFC organization a chance and see where it would lead them. The Northborough chaplain was assigned to a family and remained with them throughout the entire incident and on through the funerals.

The newest member of the MCFC assisted in the family tent, visited with some of the firefighters on the scene, and sat in on something that was new to him: a CISM demobilization.

Once his chief found out that his chaplain was at the scene, he gave him an old chaplain's bunker coat, some boots, gloves, and a red helmet with a fire chaplain insignia on it. At least he looked the part, to some degree. The deacon/chaplain from the nearby town kept going back to the site and remained there until the last firefighter was taken out. He assisted with two removals.

It was a moving experience to be called by a chief to escort the remains, which were in a body bag and "Stokes" basket, to a waiting ambulance. All the men that were present lined up in two rows which ran from the point where the remains were found and over to the ambulance. Prayers were said by another chaplain. Hand salutes were given. The remains were carried out with dignity. Amen.

This experience was the rejuvenation of the "banquet chaplain." Out of this terrible loss of lives came the rising phoenix of a chaplain who now felt that he was worth something, and could do more to assist at fires. He attended meetings of the MCFC and found out that they responded to fire, accident, and disaster scenes, and were right at the front lines, ready to assist in any way possible.

The deacon/chaplain also found out he could take classes so that his skills in crisis intervention and stress management could be more effective. The nice thing was that the Corps and the state's Department of Fire Services would cover the costs of instruction. "Where do I sign and where and when is the first course being offered?" were the questions that bolted out of his mouth. He soon got brochures, went on-line, and found out exactly what the classes were all about.

COURTESY OF THE WORCESTER TELEGRAM & GAZETTE

DEACON TONY SUROZENSKI

79

WHAT IS ALL THAT CISM STUFF, ANYWAY?

The first thing that popped up on the screen of his computer was the organization known as the International Critical Incident Stress Foundation or CISF, and the courses were about Critical Incident Stress Management, CISM. He found out that classes included Basic, Advanced, Peer Counseling/Crisis Intervention, Suicide Prevention Intervention and Postvention, Pastoral Crisis Intervention, and many others that would be beneficial, not only for a fire chaplain but also for a deacon in ministry. And so, he began to take one after another, eager to learn more and more.

It was there that he realized that what he had suppressed so many years ago. The story of the young boy who got hit by a car while running out in front of an ice cream truck surfaced in his mind as clearly as if it had happened just yesterday. He had thought that he had put it behind him, but that was not the case. The chaplain dealt with it for the first time in all those years, and was able to breathe a sigh of relief when he found out that this was normal, and that it was okay now.

He wondered: how many others were in the same predicament? He thought: how many guys bent their elbows and talked about the fire/incident calls but never really got over them? They just buried them deep within themselves. Could this be problematic for some? The answer was yes, and he concluded that that was why CISM was so important in the emergency services.

Because the chaplain was answering second alarm assignments, which meant that the fire was quite serious, he began to see how important it was to pay attention to the body language of the firefighters, their facial expressions, and their words as he approached them on the scene and back at the firehouse. Not everyone was affected the same way, and in most cases, no one appeared to be affected at all. However, there were times when some were affected and they were in need of CISM. Usually, the guys were affected because the incident involved a death or serious injury. When it involved one of their own comrades, it was very apparent that they all were affected to some degree and some more seriously than others. In this case, the chaplain would approach the incident commander or chief, and let him know that he should call for a "defusing" or a "debriefing."

How does the chaplain conclude that more help is needed? One obvious sign is what has been known for many years as "the thousand yard stare." The person affected appears to have a blank look on their face and seems to be staring way off into the distance. Often, if one were to wave their hand in front of that person, they wouldn't even flinch, and they seem to be absorbed in deep thought. This body language signal indicates help is needed.

In order to help this individual, one first tries to stabilize them by getting them away from the incident, and telling them that they could use a short break from the action. Then one acknowledges that something is going on by asking them what is happening with them at that particular moment. One could also ask, what is the worst part of this situation right now? Another question could be, what do you think will help you at this time?

After the person responds, the next step is to facilitate the situation by framing their reactions as a normal thought process, and assist in identifying the nature of the crisis. This is then followed by words of encouragement. Then an assessment is made of the person's ability to function and cope with that situation. The CISM trained person assesses the person's speech, emotions, appearance, and alertness. If all appears to be well, they may be able get back to doing what they were trained to do. If not, they may be referred to sources with more experience in handling stress.

Often, it is obvious that several of those on the scene of a tragic event need more than just one-on-one assistance. This calls for a meeting with a team of CISM trained people. This is known as a defusing. The defusing is most beneficial if it takes place right after the incident. Team members are usually made up of peers. They introduce themselves and try to put the event in context; then the event is summarized and the facilitator talks about possible effects, the normalcy of reactions, that all present belong there, that individuals should speak for themselves, and that this is not a critique. The emphasis is on confidentiality. If someone in the group is not supposed to be there, such as another firefighter or officer who was not at the event, they are asked to leave. All present are considered equals with no rank involved, and all may speak freely.

Then the exploration session begins, with each member stating their name, the job that they performed, and what happened. Then information is given by the facilitator and/or other team members about how abnormal events can create natural reactions that people may be experiencing. They are told what to look for as signs of normal stress reactions; that time is needed to overcome those reactions; that diet and exercise is important; that maintaining routine is good, which could include work, rest, and leisure activity; and to look after one another. More helpful information is given, before there are any final questions. A plan of action is given with the assurance that help is always available. If the team recognizes that anyone in the group needs further assistance, a debriefing, which is more involved, could follow within a day or two. The team for a debriefing includes a mental health person along with peers and a chaplain.

CALLED TO SERVE

RECHARGED WITH CISM AND BACK IN SERVICE

The chaplain really ate this CISM stuff up. He became part of a team in Central Massachusetts and continued to answer alarms and calls for assistance with a new enthusiasm. He once again felt like he was doing something worthwhile, and was truly of help on the fire scene as well as during a debriefing. There were several occasions where his services were called upon throughout the county. He also was involved in some pre-incident education for trainees in other fire departments as well as his own. But most of his assistance was with individual, one-on-one incidents either during a fire or shortly thereafter.

Being a former captain of a ladder company was a big help, as firefighters felt more comfortable with him once they knew that he was a firefighter. They didn't have to be on their best behavior just because the fire chaplain was on scene. Oh, they slipped in a few profanities, some "F" words quite often, and it was comical when they would apologize for what came out of their mouths. "Sorry chap." "Sorry chap." That was repeated quite often by many.

The "chap" would simply reply that it sure wasn't the first time that he had ever heard those words, and that it wouldn't make him blush. At times, he would even add that he didn't think they would go to hell for using those words. However, every so often when the chaplain heard the use of the name of Jesus in a condescending way, he would remark about it. He even would involve some humor if one of the guys was using "Jesus Christ" in almost every sentence. The chaplain would energetically turn from side to side, lift up his head,

83

look around and say, "Where did he go?" When the guys would say, "Who?" The chaplain would reply, "Jesus Christ. You keep saying his name so much that I thought He was here and I missed the second coming." They got the message and once again a "sorry chap" came forth.

The CISM training was truly a "Godsend" for the chaplain for it combined his pastoral skills with the psychological aspects of CISM. It helped not only during incidents of structure fires where people were seriously injured or where there was a death involved, or in serious motor vehicle accidents, but also in his diaconal ministry. There were times when he would be called to the hospital or home of a parishioner who was suffering from a serious injury, or loss of a loved one, or who had just found out that they had cancer. The CISM training was of extreme value in each case.

The techniques could be applied to any situation involving stress related incidents. It came under the auspices of the CISM course called Pastoral Crisis Intervention or PCI. The chaplain realized the importance of this training and felt that anyone in ministry should be exposed to it, so he applied to the ICISF leaders to become an instructor. He held his first class several months after he completed the training for PCI.

Anyone who may be interested in finding out more about ICISF may simply contact the International Critical Incident Stress Foundation, Inc. at 3290 Pine Orchard Lane, Suite 106, Ellicott City, Md. 20142. Also, contact may be made via their web site at www. icisf.org.

9-11-01 THE BEGINNING OF THE END?

Just about everyone in the United States remembers where they were on that tragic day of 9-11-01. The fire chaplain was at the rectory where he served as deacon. A phone call came in to turn on the television because something terrible had just happened at the World Trade Center. The staff immediately went into the room with the television, and the telecast showed the first plane slamming into the north tower.

All were awestruck and couldn't believe their eyes. Everyone thought that it must be an advertisement for a new movie, or how could a tragic accident like this take place? Then the information began to roll in that this was for real, and not an accident.

Then the second plane crashed into the south tower. Two planes. Certainly this was no accident. This had to have been the act of terrorists or some really crazy people. The chaplain immediately had a sentence enter his mind that he would never forget. It echoed over and over just as clear as the first time, and it was scary. The sentence was, "Now, it begins." Did this mean that this was the beginning of the end of time as we know it? He didn't want to think about it. But the words, "It could be," kept entering his thoughts.

Deacon Tony Surozenski

LOGAN COMES FIRST

Once he got over the shock, he immediately got on the phone and contacted the Chief Chaplain of the Massachusetts Corps of Fire Chaplains to let him know that if he was needed for anything, he would be available. Shortly thereafter, the chaplain received a call to report to Logan Airport. At Logan, he and other chaplains from the MCFC would be present for the families and friends of those who were on the flights that crashed into the Twin Towers.

Immediately, he contacted his wife who had been watching television and witnessed the horror. He informed her of where he was going and what he would be doing. They both prayed. They prayed for all who were lost and for the families who were left behind. They prayed for comfort, peace, wisdom, and understanding, because there would be no other way to deal with this tragedy without the help of our God. They also prayed for a safe trip to Boston and for the chaplain to be able to do his best to assist those who lost their loved ones.

The trip into Boston took about an hour, and with the help of a red light in his vehicle and his identification as a fire chaplain, he was able to maneuver into the hotel parking area and was waved on by security to a good parking spot. The MCFC had set up a receiving station for chaplains on the first floor of the hotel so it was easy for the chaplain to get his identification badge and move into the area where the families were located. Once there, his training and pastoral instincts kicked in, and he walked into one of the reception areas and began to survey the situation.

He teamed up with another chaplain and they moved about the area. They began to be present to those in need and to communicate with them. Most of the time the communication involved spending time just listening, since not much can be said in tragedies such as this. "I'm sorry for your loss" is about all one can say. The rest involves listening carefully to what people say, and acknowledging their stories and the pain that they feel. "I can understand your pain" is not a good thing to say because no one except the person who is experiencing the pain knows exactly what it is like. One can empathize but only to a certain extent. Saying things like "they are in a better place" is not good to say even if one believes strongly that they are. Most often a person who has lost someone would rather have them right there with them, even if they believe that their loved one is truly in a better place. Unless the bereaved person makes a statement like that themselves, it is never good to say that. To acknowledge it is one thing: to state it is another.

The chaplain sat with several families and offered condolences. All were thankful for the presence of the chaplains. As the chaplain rose from one table, he would scan the room to see how things were going. When he noticed that people were left alone, he would walk over and acknowledge their loss, and would ask if they would like to talk about what was going through their minds. If they said, "no." he would move on, after he told them that he and others would be available if they needed to talk.

On one occasion, he rose and noticed a young woman who appeared to be by herself and was just glancing around the room with a sad-looking expression on her face. The chaplain went over to her and introduced himself. They both sat down and she began to open up to this stranger. Her major concern was that her good friend was on one of those planes, and she wondered if it was possible that she was in heaven. When asked why her friend might not be, the young lady responded, "because we are in a loving relationship and I was told that homosexuals can't get to heaven." The chaplain asked where she had heard that and she responded, "The church that I once belonged to."

The chaplain realized that this was not the time to go through a theological dissertation. He simply began to talk about God's love for all people, and that it is an unconditional love. He also told her that only God knew what was in their minds and hearts as far as their loving relationship was concerned, and that no mortal has a right to judge whether a person is to go to heaven or hell. That judgment is left to God alone.

He asked her if she felt that her friend led a good life and loved God and God's people and she answered yes. He said, "With that in mind, where do you think your loving friend should be?" She said that she "would like to think that she is in Heaven." He followed with, "Then hold that thought in your heart and rely on the love and mercy of God and don't let anyone else try to convince you of anything else." He reiterated that God was all-loving and all-merciful, and that only God can pass judgment on us.

With tears in her eyes, and a smile on her face, she exuded a sense of comfort and peace. She and the chaplain hugged each other. She thanked him and they parted. To this day, the chaplain does not remember who she was, but prays that she is at peace and living out her life loving God and God's people to the best of her ability.

The next day brought many of the same experiences meeting with families. Many families were frustrated because there were no new reports from officials at Logan. The chaplain held a prayer service of remembrance. Expressions of sadness and disbelief were present on the faces of all. By Thursday of that week, not many families were reporting to the hotel at the airport. Many returned to their homes in anguish with little relief or hope of their loved ones being returned whole.

The chaplains could only do so much; the grieving process had begun. Only time would heal. Hopefully, some pain was relieved. Prayer was all that one could continue to offer for the repose of the souls and for the relief of pain and sorrow that filled those who suffered losses.

THE CALL COMES TO ASSIST AT GROUND ZERO

A call came from the International Association of Firefighters (IAFF) for chaplains to assist at Ground Zero. The Chief Chaplain sent one of MCFC's finest to New York to find out exactly what was needed for numbers of chaplains and what they would be doing. He left immediately. The chaplain from Attleboro, Massachusetts met with the incident commanders who were in charge of staging personnel for Ground Zero. He phoned the Chief Chaplain and said that they would need as many chaplains as possible to get down there as soon as possible. At first, the assistance was to involve delivering death notifications to the families of firefighters who had lost their loved ones in the WTC tragedy.

Arrangements were made by the chaplain from Northborough, Massachusetts for the use of passenger vans, which were to leave from the State Police barracks in Sturbridge as early as that Sunday afternoon. Phone calls went out to ten Corps members who said that they would be available to go.

The deacon/fire chaplain, and teacher who had retired in June, was at a meeting after celebrating baptisms. He received a phone call from his wife that he needed to get home ASAP because he was being deployed to New York. He said that he would have to start packing as soon as he got home. His loving, understanding wife told him that his clothes and all other necessary medications and toiletries were already packed, and that all he needed was his turn-out gear and anything else that he would need to take as chaplain.

DEACON TONY SUROZENSKI

He immediately ended the meeting and returned home to finish the packing. All that was left was to be sure that he had his turn out-gear together in his duffle bag and his Class A uniform in its garment bag. The phone kept ringing constantly as family members called to wish him well, those who could went over to the house to see him off. It was late Sunday afternoon when he arrived at the State Police barracks. One large van was packed. Prayers were said by all present. The chaplains who remained in Massachusetts waved to the contingent of ten as their van departed for New York.

No one really knew what to expect once they got into the city, and everyone was anxious and concerned. They were told that we were at war and anything could happen. The chaplains entertained thoughts of more hijacked planes coming in and being used as bombs. How safe was it? This was a question that no one could really answer.

The deacon/chaplain was kind of a jokester and occasionally he blurted out a series of jokes to take everyone's mind off the upcoming situation. They couldn't kick him out of the van, so they listened. All survived the joke ordeal and it did succeed in its objective, at least temporarily.

They finally arrived at the staging area around midnight. As soon as they arrived, they were asked to have two of the chaplains go down to the morgue at Ground Zero. Delivering death notifications appeared to be on the back burner. It looked like a whole new experience was before them. Two went off. The rest settled in at the Hilton Hotel on the Avenue of the Americas and Fifty Third Street. The deacon/chaplain prayed the evening prayer of the Divine Office and tried to get some sleep. Several chaplains crowded into one room. At least they were able to move about and clean up. Sleep finally came.

The next day, two more chaplains were sent to the morgue. It appeared as though it would be twelve-hour shifts for everyone, with off time being spent at rest or sleep or visiting with folks right around the hotel area. Debriefings were held by CISM teams. The chaplains also did their own debriefings with those chaplains who came off the pile/morgue area; they would sit and talk about what they did while at Ground Zero.

Most everyone told of the many body bags and buckets of body parts and remains that came through the makeshift morgue. At first it was just an area with plywood benches supported by two by four wooden legs. Later it developed into a receiving tent, a preliminary autopsy-type tent, and an exit area that led to waiting ambulances and refrigeration vehicles. Ambulances and the other vehicles then took their contents to the hospital morgues. Contents? The word, contents, seemed to be a bit impersonal because the pails and bags often contained fingertips, hands, bones, organs, feet, arms, and legs, but all were treated with utmost dignity.

Every little bag and bucket was treated as if it were a full-sized person. Every body, the parts of bodies, and debris containing parts were first brought into the receiving tent, and the locations where they were found were recorded. Then there was silence as the chaplains prayed over the remains. The remains were then accompanied to the next section of the tent, where medical examiners continued their investigations.

Rescue/recovery members brought the body bags and buckets/pails into the receiving area and placed them on the floor or table. Identification was given as to civilian, fire, police, federal, or court, etc, and a location was given as to where they were found, in a building, street, or ramp, etc. All the information was recorded on a tape. The tape was placed on the bag and the information was also recorded in a book.

Then workers all paused, and the chaplains prayed. They asked God's blessing upon each bag, and at times, early on, all were sprinkled with holy water. The fire chaplains, when members of the emergency services were identified, would have the rescue/recovery members stand at attention and hold a right hand salute while a prayer was offered. Then the body would be taken to the next room for further examination, and as in the case of a firefighter's body, was then accompanied to an ambulance, and then taken to the official hospital morgue. Dignity and respect were always the order of the day for all who worked in the morgue.

Every so often, one of the chaplains would take a break from the morgue and walk around the area and even over to the pile where the pails and bags were coming from. He or she would talk with the rescue/recovery personnel and offer comfort where and when they could, and as best that they could under the stressful circumstances. Simple presence seemed to be so important to the workers. So many would nod, smile, and say thanks for being there. Eye contact was essential along with the occasional pat on the back as they passed through the area. All gave signs of appreciation.

During the deacon/chaplain's shift, on the eighteenth of September, he and his Lutheran chaplain friend had the honor of praying for a captain of a ladder company and a battalion commander, as well as many others. Because he himself was once a captain of a ladder company, he really took it to heart in a special way. While the members held a right hand salute, he not only prayed for that captain but also included the captain's family and men who served with him. He then accompanied the men to the next section of the morgue, and remained with them, following them out to the waiting ambulance, where he shed a tear along with those who knew the fallen hero.

He was Captain Timothy Stackpole, who had been recently promoted to captain not long before the attack on 9-11-01. His friend, Dennis Cross, the Battalion Commander, was found right near him. The names of both the captain and the commander escaped the chaplain for some time but they came to light after reading a book about the victims of that tragic day.

At approximately the same time that the planes went into the Towers one week earlier, men at the staging area were getting ready to relieve those who were on the pile. The deacon/chaplain walked around and was conversing with those who were ready to go on the rescue/recovery mission. Some were wondering if they could have a brief moment of silence or prayer before they moved on. The chaplain heard it and moved over to the shift commander and asked for a brief moment of his time.

The chaplain asked the commander if it would be possible, before they left for the pile, to say a brief prayer. The commander looked at his watch and responded with "Let's not wait. Let's do it now." He called the men to attention and announced that the chaplain would offer a brief prayer in remembrance of all who were lost and still missing. The chaplain offered that prayer, along with a prayer for the safety of all who were working at the scene. The deacon/chaplain felt that it was a great honor and privilege to be able to do that for New York's bravest. The staging area was moved later that day, because it was too close to the morgue. No one needed to be reminded of the horror of the pails and bags.

Stories get exaggerated at times and even made up, and Tuesday was no exception. Someone received a message from a person on the pile about a chaplain who was jumping up and down on the pile and seemed to be out of control. He was to be removed immediately. Reference was made to either the deacon/chaplain or his Lutheran friend.

When they both arrived back at headquarters, they were immediately met by the heads of a Massachusetts CISM team for a debriefing. When asked about the jumping up and down, both were highly insulted that anyone could think that of them. The Lutheran chaplain was a World War II Navy veteran and an experienced fire chaplain. The other chaplain had been a fire captain and had close to thirty years experience in the fire service. Both had witnessed many deaths and served at many funerals throughout their clergy careers. To this day, no one knows how that story got out or if there was actually someone who did experience that bizarre behavior.

That evening, all the chaplains were to get dressed in their Class A uniforms and attend a gathering with families of firefighters who lost their loved ones at Ground Zero. Not all were able to attend. Two were on duty at the morgue and two figured that they had better get some well-deserved rest and be ready for whatever tomorrow would bring.

Wednesday was a day to get FEMA identification badges for those who were not able to get them earlier due to their work at the site or at firehouses. Once the identification badges were received they felt more comfortable working in the area. During their free time, several chaplains, who were not on duty, walked around the Times Square area, went over to St. Patrick's Cathedral and were able to get in some other sight-seeing experiences, which served as a type of therapy. It was never all play because they stopped and talked with many New Yorkers who lived and worked there. Some wore face masks due to the ever-present haze of dust particles that came from the fallen towers. Just about everyone who spoke with the chaplains was still in a state of disbelief at the events of 9-11. All were appreciative of he chaplains' being there and doing their work.

The most emotional times for the deacon/chaplain were on the return trips from Ground Zero. This was so because of the lines of people on the sides of the roads who held up large "Thank You" signs and yelled out words of appreciation and thanks. Many also held out bottles of water, soda, and juice. The applause of the bystanders brought tears to his eyes. He hoped that they realized how much it meant to those who worked at Ground Zero. They are still in his prayers to this day and will be for as long as he is able to pray.

A second 12 hour shift was in order for the deacon/chaplain and his Lutheran friend along with a deputy chief chaplain who was an Episcopalian priest. Back to the morgue they went to pray over more body parts and to give support wherever it was needed. This time, with three chaplains on duty, it was easier for one of them to move about the area. They took turns as time permitted. At one point, all three were able to get up into the building that overlooked the pile and got a bird's eye view of all that was going on. It was still a surreal event in each of their minds.

During one of the breaks, the fire commissioner was on the scene and thanked all present for their efforts. When he noticed the chaplains, he walked over to them and talked about the horror that all were witnessing. He also asked what so many ask in times such as these, "How did God allow all this suffering to happen?" The deacon/chaplain remembered what he once heard and told him: "God never promised us that we would never suffer but He did promise us that we would never suffer alone and that He would be there in our suffering." The chaplain said that "God was in every person who has reached out to help since the beginning of the rescue operations. He was in all the men and women who are still offering their services. And He is crying along with us and offering us comfort through those who are present."

The commissioner seemed to understand and even though the words did not take away the pain, they did appear to be of some comfort.

From the very beginning people were pulling together to help each other, and each day thereafter was no different. Love, kindness, goodness, helpfulness, caring and gratefulness are words that could be used to describe all who were on and off the scene. More people with God-like love came forward during those difficult days, weeks, and months following 9-11. The chaplains stood in awe, for what they had preached to so many about God-like love, in each of their own congregations over the years, was visible to them at Ground Zero.

CROSS AT GROUND ZERO

DEACON TONY SUROZENSKI

THEY ALL CAME TO SERVE

COURTESY OF MASSACHUSETTS CORPS OF FIRE CHAPLAINS

THOSE WHO SERVED WILL NEVER FORGET

Courtesy Massachusetts Corps of Fire Chaplains

Deacon Tony Surozenski

THE NEED NEVER SEEMS TO END

Membership in the MCFC leads chaplains to all parts of the state of Massachusetts and also to communities throughout the United States. Wherever there is a need for a chaplain, services are available through the Massachusetts Corps of Fire Chaplains. It wasn't too long after 9-11 that other emergencies broke out where the Corps was called and the deacon/chaplain was available to serve.

One particular incident was on a Veteran's Day Weekend. The MCFC was called out to a mill complex fire in Pawtucket, Rhode Island. It just so happened that the deacon/chaplain and his wife were at a conference in Newport, R.I. and while watching a news break on television, the call came to see who was available. It also happened to be in the deacon/chaplain's wife's home town, and only two streets away from where she grew up.

How could she say no to his responding to that call? Besides, she was in good hands with other deacons and their wives, who would be going to a dinner theater. He promised that he would try to get back as soon as possible.

The fire was devastating, with damage to surrounding homes caused by winds that carried fire brands to rooftops. The surrounding fire departments were busy extinguishing those fires while the major attack was on the mill complex. The chaplains were present in the rehabilitation area to talk with anyone who seemed to want to share the experience or to talk about anything else that was on their minds.

Fortunately, there were more chaplains than needed, and the deacon/chaplain was able to get back to his wife and friends and catch the end of the show back in Newport.

A more difficult call came in not long after that incident: the Warwick, Rhode Island "Station Club" fire, where hundreds lost their lives. The deacon/chaplain was fortunate that he was only involved with the second shift of chaplains that came in to relieve those who were there from the onset. "Fortunate" also because he did not experience the stress load of those who served while bodies were being removed. He did not experience the sights and smells of this type of tragedy.

However, this chaplain had the opportunity and privilege to escort the last body to the ambulance and to offer silent prayers as they closed the doors and left for the morgue. He also was able to talk with several who had experienced the tragedy. There were many instances of the classic "thousand yard stare." For those who experienced the "stare," listening was key on the chaplain's part. There were the usual questions about "Why did this have to happen? And "How could God let this happen?"

He could not give any concrete answers. Can there ever be any during the immediate time frame of the incident? However, the chaplains' presence was appreciated. All were still under the "first aid" aspect of stress, and debriefings were to follow within the next several days. The Corps' usual question is "Where will we be called to next?" May God continue to be with us as we serve those in need.

Deacon Tony Surozenski

LIFE IS TOO SHORT –
MIGHT AS WELL HAVE ADRINK

At one point in time, shortly after the events of 9-11-01, the deacon/chaplain looked back at all that he had experienced and for the first time in 14 years of sobriety thought that it would be okay for him to have a drink now and then. He talked to his wife about it and told her that he wanted to have a drink with her from time to time but that he did not want to go back to his old habits of drinking day in and day out. He asked her to watch him and to be sure that she would tell him if he was overdoing it. His loving wife said that she would and so he did.

He started by only drinking while on vacation. Then it went to holidays as well. That turned into weekends. Weekends turned into weekdays. All drinking was done responsibly and no driving was involved after more than two drinks. The deacon/chaplain was really enjoying his newfound freedom to drink like others and not get himself into trouble. He could even go out, have wine with his wife over dinner and even a Scotch before dinner. Within the course of an hour or so, he was still "good to go" with no urge to have more than the two at the restaurant.

Now, the problem was that he began to notice that he was beginning to look forward to having the drinks. He noticed that he couldn't wait to get home to have a drink ready when his wife arrived home from work. He enjoyed having more than two with her while relaxing in front of the fireplace and that it even improved their romance. The red flags began to wave and finally one day he thought, "What if I got a call to go out to a fire or a CISM call?" What would have to happen is that he would have to say no and call for a replacement. Then, if something happened to the replacement, how could he face himself or others?

The deacon/chaplain decided that if he could do it for 14 years, he could do it again. If he didn't need alcohol for all that time, why did he need it now? And so, he quit one more time and hoped that with the grace of his "Higher Power," his God, he would remain alcohol-free for the rest of his life. It would be difficult, though especially when the "Life is too short, so why not have fun?" thought kicks in; and when the one who drinks is finally drinking responsibly. What is the big deal?

The big deal is that volumes of written testimony and research tell the one involved that this type of thinking leads to problems with health of mind and body. So, the struggle would continue as the chaplain takes it "one day at a time."

A HOUSE OF CARDS

If one were to build a house of cards with the fifty two cards that are in a deck of playing cards, how many cards could one pull out before the house collapses? A lot would depend upon a variety of factors, but the reader might imagine that it usually doesn't take many, and that all that is necessary might be just one to have the house of cards, that may have taken quite some time to build, come tumbling down. The chaplain/deacon or deacon/chaplain (because the roles flip flop and blend so very often) didn't come to realize that he himself was like a house of cards with fate ready to pull on one card.

The deacon/chaplain was supposed to have been retired from his teaching career of thirty-six years in June of 2001. He did retire, but slowly took on more responsibilities that led to more than forty hours a week of time spent in diaconal ministry and his outreach ministry as fire chaplain.

The cards seemed to line up this way: he worked as Assistant to the Director of the Diaconate formation program on Monday and Wednesday evenings from approximately six in the evening to about nine or so. On Monday, Tuesday, and Wednesday he worked at the rectory as a deacon, where his duties included visiting the homebound, setting up baptismal preparations for families, counseling those who were in need, preaching at a Mass during the week, serving at funerals and graveside services when necessary, presiding at a communion service at a rehabilitation facility, and a few other things here and there. On Thursdays he spent time in the diocesan Tribunal Office assisting folks with marital issues. On alternate Saturdays and every Sunday he served at Masses.

Some of this changed when he was appointed Director of the Diaconate Program for the diocese. Added responsibilities included taking care of over sixty deacons throughout the diocese, and now running the formation program which operated on a Tri-semester academic model. This program had several formation classes going on at the same time, with the average time from start to ordination being five years. This also included the preparation of budgets and other administrative duties.

Other cards from the deck lined up in this fashion: the fire chaplaincy for his own department which included answering second alarm assignments (the fire is really raging), meeting with firefighters from time to time, setting up prayer services, and serving at liturgies for various functions and the like.

The cards of membership in the Massachusetts Corps of Fire Chaplains were stacked with District Coordinator, board of directors' member, and later a shift to Chief Chaplain's Aide, including directors' meetings, local meetings, and general meetings.

The Critical Incident Stress Management cards covered monthly meetings, conferences, trainings, and educational workshops. Pastoral Crisis Intervention Instructor was another card from the deck.

Family responsibilities as husband, father, and grandfather, along with the needs of taking care of a house and yard, made up the final group. Balancing all the cards is the key to a solid house of cards.

The base is supposed to be made up of family and prayer. Shuffle the cards and it can look pretty scary as to where the priorities get dealt for stacking. One card pulled to move around and get it right might be the one that topples the whole stack.

It just so happened that an unexpected card got pulled from the house. This card involved a health issue, not of a serious nature but just enough to make the deacon/chaplain think about his "house of cards." It happened on a warm summer afternoon in July at approximately 3:15 P.M. on Friday the 13th.

You know who, the former Ladder One captain, the deacon/chaplain, finished painting the south side of his storage shed and was taking down his makeshift staging when he noticed that he had missed a piece of molding under the eave of the roof. It was too high to reach with his outstretched hand so he set up a step ladder to make it easier to get to. Once it was set and tested for balance he began to climb it with the paint can and brush in one hand.

As he turned for a better position, he slipped. His body weight shifted and the ladder began to move out from under him. As it began to fall over, he decided that it would be best to jump off. That he did, but did not realize that only one foot would land on the softness of the grass and soil while the other was headed for a concrete stepping stone. He did realize it when the excruciating pain radiated up from his heel and into his right leg. Beads of sweat poured all over his body along with the sense of nausea and dizziness.

The former ladder man thought that it would go away so if he rested a while, all would be better. This was negated as he lifted himself up and tried to apply pressure to the injured foot. The pain never ceased to penetrate the heel and lower leg. He thought, "Damn, this is a hospital event." He couldn't make it go away. He couldn't pray it away. No doubt there was serious injury to that right foot. The best he could hope for was a bad sprain or bruise. As he began to crawl to the house for help, his wife noticed that something definitely was wrong and that he wasn't crawling around looking for a lost putty knife, brush, or nail.

The trip to the hospital only took five minutes, and as luck would have it, an orthopedic surgeon was in house. The x-rays and CT-scan showed three breaks in the calcaneous heel bone which would need to be set with two screws and the incision with seventeen staples. That surgery took place the following Monday. The recuperation period would be at least six to eight weeks with crutches, a walker, and eventually a cane.

The jokester part of the deacon/chaplain said, while in the emergency room, " At least he got a good break having the orthopedic surgeon present, and now he will be living proof that he is really 'screwed up.'" Now, he couldn't kick about that, could he?

TIME TO RESHUFFLE THE DECK

With a forced vacation of four weeks off one's feet, and with nothing to do but sit around, one has a lot of time to think, pray, and reflect on the events of the past several days as well as those that went into building the house of cards. "Stop and smell the roses" was one thing that popped into his mind as he sat outside in the warmth of the summer breeze that was filled with the scent of flowers.

As he observed the flowers in the flower garden he noticed the buzzing activity of the bumble bees and an occasional visit of a humming bird. "Wow, what activity, what power, what beauty, right here in my own back yard;" was the next thought that passed through his mind. This led to deeper thought, prayer, and meditation as to who he was, what he was doing, and where this was leading him.

He could not continue to do everything and do it well. So, after much prayer and discussion with his wife, the deacon/chaplain decided to cut back one day at the rectory and add a day to the Office of the Diaconate. He had already cut back on the CISM team meetings and would also have to cut back on other meetings. However, no way could he give up going out on second alarm assignments with the fire service. He was still in love with those big red trucks and those who rode on them. He simply couldn't think of leaving the department without a chaplain. Thoughts of leaving in the future had entered his mind but that would be in the future. Could this particular shuffle do the trick? Who could he recommend as the next chaplain for the department? Only time would tell.

THEY WILL ALWAYS BE REMEMBERED

CourtEsy of The Catholic Free Press of the Diocese of Worcester

WE HONOR OUR FALLEN HEROES

COURTESY OF THE CATHOLIC FREE PRESS OF THE DIOCESE OF WORCESTER

DEACON TONY SUROZENSKI

107

GODS'S GRACES HELP TO ENDURE

EPILOGUE

Since the reshuffling time, the deacon/chaplain broke a digit on the index finger of his right hand, and had two bouts with kidney stones. Splitting wood with mauls and sledgehammers can sometimes lead to accidents, and that is just what happened with the finger.

Anyone who has experienced kidney stones realizes that it is no fun at all, and that following the doctor's orders with regard to diet is necessary even if it means giving up things that one likes.

Were those yet other signs to slow down and rethink the future? It would appear that he must take time to do just that. His thoughts are centering upon teaching and preaching within the context of his vocation as deacon and as chaplain. A continued blending of the two may just be what The Doctor is ordering. The pace could be slower, but the results could be greater for the one who serves. Hopefully, the results will always be of benefit to all, but especially to those who serve on those big red trucks. (Or whatever color they could be.)

DEACON TONY SUROZENSKI

DEACON TONY SUROZENSKI – FIRE CHAPLAIN

ABOUT THE AUTHOR

The author lives with his wife in Webster Massachusetts, serves as Fire Chaplain for the Webster Fire Department, is Chief Chaplain's Aide for the Massachusetts Corps of Fire Chaplains, is also the Director for the Office of the Diaconate of the Diocese of Worcester, Massachusetts, and is an instructor for the International Critical Incident Stress Foundation, Inc. and is approved to teach Pastoral Crisis Intervention I & II and Emotional and Spiritual Care in Disasters. He is also a member of the Worcester Central Massachusetts Critical Incident Stress Management Team.

He earned a B.S. & M. Ed. Degree in Secondary Education from Worcester State College and has "Master Catechist" certification from the Diocese of Worcester.

HELPFUL RESOURCES IN TIME OF TROUBLE:

A.A. WORLD SERVICES, INC.
WWW.AA.ORG 212-870-3400

AL-ANON & ALATEEN
WWW.AL-ANON.ALATEEN.ORG 888-425-2666

AMERICAN RED CROSS
WWW.REDCROSS.ORG 800-733-2767

CATHOLIC RELIEF SERVICES
WWW.CRS.ORG 888-277-7575 EMAIL- INFO@CRS.ORG

INTERNATIONAL CRITICAL INCIDENT STRESS FOUNDATION, INC.
(ICISF) WWW.ICISF.ORG 410-750-9600
EMAIL- INFO@ICISF.ORG
EMERGENCY PHONE-410-313-2473

INTERNATIONAL COMMITTEE OF THE RED CROSS
WWW.ICRC.ORG +41 (22) 734 60 01 EMAIL-WEBMASTER@ICRC.ORG

QPR INSTITUTE
(QUESTION-PERSUADE-REFER)
(SUICIDE INTERVENTION PREVENTION PROGRAM)
WWW.QPRINSTITUTE.COM 888-726-7926 509-536-5100

SUICIDE INTERVENTION-PREVENTION
WWW.SUICIDOLOGY.ORG 800-273-8255

SALVATION ARMY INTERNATIONAL
WWW.SALVATIONARMY.ORG

SALVATION ARMY U.S.A.
WEBMASTER@USN.SALVATIONARMY.ORG

RESOURCES SPECIFIC TO EMERGENCY SERVICE PERSONNEL:

INTERNATIONAL ASSOCIATION OF FIREFIGHTERS
(IAFF) WWW.IAFF.ORG 202-737-8484

MASSACHUSETTS CORPS OF FIRE CHAPLAINS
WWW.MASSFIRECHAPLAINS.COM
774-696-4587 EMAIL-JTILBE@COMCAST.NET

NATIONAL VOLUNTEER FIRE FIGHTER COUNCIL
WWW.NVFC.ORG 888-275-6832
EMAIL-NVFCOFFICE@NVFC.ORG

ON-SITE ACADEMY GARDNER, MASSACHUSETTS
WWW.ONSITEACADEMY.ORG 978-874-0177

SANDY SCERRA MA PEER SUPPORT NETWORK,
COORDINATOR ICISF, FACULTY
978.808.7454 (C)

Other Titles of Interest

C. S. Lewis

Speaking of Jack: A C. S. Lewis Discussion Guide
Will Vaus

C. S. Lewis Societies have been forming around the world since the first one started in New York City in 1969. Will Vaus has started and led three groups himself. *Speaking of Jack* is the result of Vaus' experience in leading those Lewis Societies. Included here are introductions to most of Lewis' books as well as questions designed to stimulate discussion about Lewis' life and work. These materials have been "road-tested" with real groups made up of young and old, some very familiar with Lewis and some newcomers. *Speaking of Jack* may be used in an existing book discussion group, Sunday school class or small group, to start a C. S. Lewis Society, or as a guide to your own exploration of Lewis' books.

The Hidden Story of Narnia:
A Book-By-Book Guide to Lewis' Spiritual Themes
Will Vaus

A book of insightful commentary equally suited for teens or adults – Will Vaus points out connections between the *Narnia* books and spiritual/biblical themes, as well as between ideas in the *Narnia* books and C. S. Lewis' other books. Learn what Lewis himself said about the overarching and unifying thematic structure of the Narnia books. That is what this book explores; what C. S. Lewis called "the hidden story" of Narnia. Each chapter includes questions for individual use or small group discussion.

C. S. Lewis: His Literary Achievement
Colin Manlove

"This is a positively brilliant book, written with splendor, elegance, profundity and evidencing an enormous amount of learning. This is probably not a book to give a first-time reader of Lewis. But for those who are more broadly read in the Lewis corpus this book is an absolute gold mine of information. The author gives us a magnificent overview of Lewis' many writings, tracing for us thoughts and ideas which recur throughout, and at the same time telling us how each book differs from the others. I think it is not extravagant to call *C. S. Lewis: His Literary Achievement* a *tour de force*."

Robert Merchant, *St. Austin Review*, Book Review Editor

C. S. Lewis & Philosophy as a Way of Life: His Philosophical Thoughts
Adam Barkman

C. S. Lewis is rarely thought of as a "philosopher" per se despite having both studied and taught philosophy for several years at Oxford. Lewis's long journey to Christianity was essentially philosophical – passing through seven different stages. This 624 page book is an invaluable reference for C. S. Lewis scholars and fans alike.

C. S. Lewis: Views From Wake Forest - Essays on C. S. Lewis
Michael Travers, editor

Contains sixteen scholarly presentations from the international C. S. Lewis convention in Wake Forest, NC. Walter Hooper shares his important essay "Editing C. S. Lewis," a chronicle of publishing decisions after Lewis' death in 1963.

"Scholars from a variety of disciplines address a wide range of issues. The happy result is a fresh and expansive view of an author who well deserves this kind of thoughtful attention."
Diana Pavlac Glyer, author of *The Company They Keep*

C. S. Lewis Goes to Heaven: A Reader's Guide to The Great Divorce
David G. Clark

This is the first book devoted solely to this often neglected book and the first to reveal several important secrets Lewis concealed within the story. Lewis felt his imaginary trip to Hell and Heaven was far better than his book *The Screwtape Letters*, which has become a classic. Clark is an ordained minister who has taught courses on Lewis for more than 30 years and is a New Testament and Greek scholar with a Doctor of Philosophy degree in Biblical Studies from the University of Notre Dame. Readers will discover the many literary and biblical influences Lewis utilized in writing his brilliant novel.

Why I Believe in Narnia:
33 Reviews and Essays on the Life and Work of C.S. Lewis
James Como

Chapters range from reviews of critical books , documentaries and movies to evaluations of Lewis' books to biographical analysis.
"A valuable , wide-ranging collection of essays by one of the best informed and most accute commentators on Lewis' work and ideas."
Peter Schakel, author of *Imagination & the Arts in C.S. Lewis*

George MacDonald

Diary of an Old Soul & The White Page Poems
George MacDonald and Betty Aberlin

The first edition of George MacDonald's book of daily poems included a blank page opposite each page of poems. Readers were invited to write their own reflections on the "white page." MacDonald wrote: "Let your white page be ground, my print be seed, growing to golden ears, that faith and hope may feed." Betty Aberlin responded to MacDonald's invitation with daily poems of her own.

Betty Aberlin's close readings of George MacDonald's verses and her thoughtful responses to them speak clearly of her poetic gifts and spiritual intelligence. Luci Shaw, poet

In the Near Loss of Everything: George MacDonald's Son in America
Dale Wayne Slusser

In the summer of 1887, George MacDonald's son Ronald, newly engaged to artist Louise Blandy, sailed from England to America to teach school. The next summer he returned to England to marry Louise and bring her back to America. On August 27, 1890, Louise died leaving him with an infant daughter. Ronald once described losing a beloved spouse as "the near loss of everything". Dale Wayne Slusser unfolds this poignant story with unpublished letters and photos that give readers a glimpse into the close-knit MacDonald family. Also included is Ronald's essay about his father, *George MacDonald: A Personal Note*, plus a selection from Ronald's 1922 fable, *The Laughing Elf,* about the necessity of both sorrow and joy in life.

George MacDonald: Literary Heritage and Heirs
Roderick McGillis, editor

This collection of 14 essays sets a new standard that will influence MacDonald studies for many more years. George MacDonald experts are increasingly evaluating his entire corpus within the nineteenth century context.

This comprehensive collection represents the best of contemporary scholarship on George MacDonald. Rolland Hein, author of *George MacDonald: Victorian Mythmaker.*

Other Titles

To Love Another Person: A Spiritual Journey Through Les Miserables
John Morrison

The powerful story of Jean Valjean's redemption is beloved by readers and theater goers everywhere. In this companion and guide to Victor Hugo's masterpiece, author John Morrison unfolds the spiritual depth and breadth of this classic novel and broadway musical.

The Cat on the Catamaran: A Christmas Tale
John Martin

Here is a modern-day parable of a modern-day cat with modern-day attitudes. Riverboat Dan is a "cool" cat on a perpetual vacation from responsibility. He's *The Cat on the Catamaran* – sailing down the river of life. Dan keeps his guilty conscience from interfrering with his fun until he runs into trouble. But will he have the courage to believe that it's never too late to change course? (For ages 10 to adult)

"Cat lovers and poetry lovers alike will enjoy this whimsical story about Riverboat Dan, a philosophical cat in search of meaning."
Regina Doman, author of Angel in the Waters

Remembering Roy Campbell: The Memoirs of his Daughters, Anna and Tess
Introduction by Judith Lütge Coullie, Editor
Preface by Joseph Pearce

Anna and Teresa Campbell were the daughters of the handsome young South African poet and writer, Roy Campbell (1901-1957), and his beautiful English wife, Mary Garman. In their frank and moving memoirs, Anna and Tess recall the extraordinary, and often very difficult, lives they shared with their exceptional parents. Over 50 photos, 344 footnotes, timeline of Campbell's life, and complete index.

The Living Word of the Living God:
A Beginners Guide to Reading and Understanding the Bible
Rev. Thomas Furrer

This book is based on over 20 years experience of teaching the Bible to confirmation classes at Episcopal churches in Connecticut. Chapters from Genesis to Revelation.

CPSIA information can be obtained at www.ICGtesting.com
263489BV00001B/2/P

9 781936 294077